What people are saying…

"Terry Lee shared with our ch[illegible] son Rick's traumatic accident, and we were all blown away by her genuine conversations with God. Terry's description of clinging to God while clinging to her son's life caused us to consider God's presence in every detail of our lives. Her background with her parents, her Southern humor, and her authenticity make this a real life story I desire to hear repeatedly. Our church was applauding on its feet with gratitude for God's grace and Terry's openness."

David Hardy
Executive Pastor
Brookwood Church

Listening to the events of your life was a much-needed reminder that we all encounter impossibly difficult life trials. The details of our stories are always going to be unique, but our hurt and pain is not. Your story encouraged me to look past the pain and focus on the miracles of life. When believers join together and support one another, miracles do happen. Your story is hard evidence of this.

Brook Patterson
Greenville, SC

By: Ellen Patricia Ackerman

One scary day

One day my mom got a phone call and it was frighning. It was about my cousin, Rick Lee was in a car wreak. Ethan and I were badly sad. I got so sad I had to get to my bed. I was not doing so well. "Why couldn't it be me. Why did it have to be Rick". I said that all day lone long. It was hard for me to deal with it. I can't beleive Rick's mom could deal with it. It was good to go to school to get it off my mind. But he is as good as new in Aiken.

Ellen Ackerman
Age 8
Rick's Cousin

Desperate Cry

A Journey Through the Uncertainty of Traumatic Brain Injury

TERRY R. LEE

With Foreword by
Rick Lee

ISBN 13: 978-0-615-85225-6

To order books or schedule Terry Lee to speak at your church or event, you can contact her at:

terrylee@bellsouth.net
or
4 Belair Terrace
Aiken, SC 29801
(803) 644-0706

With overwhelming thanks to our Cedar Creek Church family, the amazing caregivers at Palmetto Health Richland Memorial Hospital and Shepherd Center.

Special thanks to:

Lonnie Gilbert (Brookwood Church) - Cover Art

Walter Ray (Cedar Creek Church) - Cover Layout

David and Amy Hardy, Gail Hendrix - Proofing and Editing

Deidre Collins and Emily Lee - Typists

Tom and Tonia McCullough - Home Group Leaders and a constant source of love and encouragement

Emily Lee (our family photographer) - Photos

"We loved you so much that we shared not only God's Good News but our own lives, too."
I Thessalonians 2:8

Contents

Foreword

On September 4, 2012 my life swerved in a direction that was unpredicted, undesired, and in many ways terrifying. But, that was also the day my life was blessed more abundantly than I could have ever imagined.

The day unfolded like any other day. I went to work, left work and then headed to my church small group. I ate, threw darts and talked Jesus with friends. I headed home around 9:30 p.m. to prepare for the following day. A day filled with the work I loved, being the youth pastor at Cedar Creek Church on the Ridge. There were no signs that anything unexpected would happen, but that is exactly what did happen.

On the way home, my truck left the road, cut down several trees, spun 180 degrees, and came to a violent stop…crushed and half submerged in a pond. The outward results of this accident were a totaled truck, broken bones, stitches, and two different forms of traumatic brain injury, but the most lasting effect of this accident is a story. A story of God's grace, love and power, but most importantly, a story of God's glory! It is my prayer that God continues to use this story, not for my glory, but to point people to Jesus and to call them into a relationship with Him.

I have the ability to write this foreword as a result of God's grace and God's grace alone. I had amazing doctors, gifted therapists and continuous support from my family and friends in the months following my accident. But, doctors did not heal me…Jesus did. I am entirely undeserving of this healing, but I am deeply grateful to a Savior and Lord who poured it out. I am eternally grateful for those of you who partnered in prayer for me while I was in the hospital and poured out love on my family in those months. I am beyond blessed to have the family that I do and beyond blessed that we have the support system in you guys that we do! Thank you so much!!!

This is not a book about Rick Lee, my family, or even my accident. It is a story of desperation, a story of hope, and a story of healing. I pray that this book, my accident and my life as a whole are tools used by God to point people to Jesus. The end goal of this book is not to make me famous, my accident famous, or my family famous. The end goal of this book, of my family, of all of creation is to make Jesus famous. He deserves glory for what happened in my accident and in the days, weeks, and months that followed… not me, not doctors, not my family, but Jesus.

It is my prayer that through Jesus' healing of my traumatic brain injury those of us who know Jesus and are saved by his grace will be reminded of the healing and reconciliation that he has already poured out in our lives. It is also my hope that those of you who do not know Jesus will get a glimpse of his redemptive story, a story that we call the Gospel. Jesus stepped in and saved me. I didn't deserve it (could never do anything to deserve it) but Jesus did it. This same Jesus is doing this every day for people with a far larger issue than traumatic brain injury. Jesus is stepping in and saving lost people, not so they can go back to life as normal, but so they can live life on a mission and have an eternity to pour back on to Jesus His value and His glory. Please allow this book to be about Jesus.

Following my accident, life sent me on a roller coaster ride. One day was great, the next I had trouble standing long enough to walk down the hallway. I would embrace the notion that I was getting better and preparing to go home, only daily to be reminded by doctors that it may be awhile before I could go. I received encouraging text messages and phone calls from friends and family, only to have to lay in bed wondering how long it would be before I could hunt or watch Clemson football with them again. As a youth pastor, I could check Facebook and see the students I was blessed to lead, but had no idea when or **IF** I would ever be able to preach or hang out with them. I was crippled with fear that my very life's calling would be stripped away as a result of a car accident and a traumatic brain injury. My life seemed to unfold as a never-ending string of question marks, a rocky streambed ever changing with the passing seconds. My life and the roller coaster it had become made me a man desperate for stability. I became a man whose only cry was, "God give me something that I can cling to that won't change tomorrow."

I had no idea how to handle the cards life had dealt me. I was a 22-year-old kid 4 months removed from graduating from Clemson University. I had just begun to get my feet wet in life. I even caught myself in the dangerous world of nearly mocking what Jesus says in The Gospel of John:

"The thief comes only to steal and kill and destroy. I came that they may have life and have it abundantly." John 10:10 (ESV)

How could Jesus say this and not stop my wreck? Did He not have the power to stop it? Did I do something so bad that I needed punishment from Him? How could I have life abundantly when I had to have someone hold me up by a belt so that I was able to walk? Nothing seemed to make sense. Life didn't seem abundant; it seemed more like hell than an abundance given by Jesus. I was filled with confusion and anger. I was lost and drowning just trying to keep my head above the water. How was I going to make anything out of myself when my life looked like this?

This last question reveals the flaw that was present in my logic. I was banking on myself being able to do anything about what had and was still happening to me. I had fallen victim to what we all do daily. I had made myself the idol and my circumstances the measure of success. I missed what was right in front of me. I can't make anything out of myself. None of us can. God is the author of time, and I had begun to second-guess Him. I was questioning the God who had created everything out of nothing. How foolish is that? I questioned if my brain would ever work again, as if I did not believe the God that created that brain from nothing was capable of healing it. My lack of trust in God and his plan put me in a dark place, and it does the same for us in everyday life. We doubt God when our paycheck doesn't seem to be enough….we doubt Him when something in life doesn't go the way we had envisioned it going. We are quick to cease worshipping and start doubting any time our road gets tougher to walk than we would like for it to be. Please understand that God is ALWAYS in control and His promises (including life abundantly) will always hold up.

Far too often we misinterpret "life abundantly" as the "American dream." We try to turn Jesus into our wingman that has our back and will fight for us instead of recognizing Him as a Savior who paid our debt and has already won the fight for us. The reality of life abundantly is that life abundantly and any life at all is impossible without Jesus. We are that desperate for Him whether we have a traumatic brain injury or not.

What I began to discover in that Atlanta hospital, and that I hope you will discover in the pages of this book, is that the measurement of abundant life is not in physical health, circumstances or possessions, but the presence of Jesus. That is what we need to desperately cry out for.

Rick Lee

Swerved off Course

Listen to my cry, for I am in desperate need.
Psalm 142:6 (NIV)

We were all glued to the television set, ironically watching one of the "Life in the Emergency Room" type dramas. As a nurse, I love watching those shows and would always try to pre-diagnose the patient before they got to the end of the episode. This episode was a great one…a young man brought in following a MVA….trauma team standing by.

"What's a MVA?" asked Katelyn.

"It stands for motor vehicle accident," I replied quickly, not wanting to miss a minute of the drama, forfeiting my chance to determine the extent of his injuries before the doctor's official diagnosis was announced.

Phillip was sideline commentating from his seat on the couch..."C-spine collar in place…order CT of the abdomen and type and cross for two units." We had watched just enough episodes and he had listened to enough of my nursing stories over the years to be hilarious.

"Be quiet!" I fussed, motioning for him to let the TV do the talking. "We are missing some of the symptoms!"

The phone began to ring in the kitchen, a huge intrusion to the drama that was unfolding in the den. I hesitated for a moment, hoping Phillip or Katelyn would move to answer it. No luck. Goodness, I thought, glancing at the clock...It's 10:45 at night, this must be a call for Phillip. I ran to the kitchen to pick up the phone, hoping the commercial break would last long enough for me to make my own diagnosis.

"Hello," I said, pausing for a minute in the kitchen to hear.

"Mrs. Lee, this is Jason. I need to speak to Pastor Phillip."

"OK, Jason. Just a minute," as I motioned for Phillip to come to the phone.

As Phillip took the phone from me, I thought about the sound of Jason's voice. It was quiet and steady, but I sensed it had a little urgency in it, as well. I have taken that kind of call many times as a pastor's wife, but I was totally un-prepared for the call we received that night. I leaned up against the kitchen counter for a minute, watching Phillip carefully as he listened to Jason on the other end of the line. Something was wrong. I was convinced of it now as I continued to watch Phillip's face.

"Oh, my God, where is he?" exclaimed Phillip. There was an ominous silence now as Phillip stood completely still. Our eyes locked and I could feel the horrifying confirmation that they were talking about one of our children. Time stood still for me. I was aware of total silence in the house now as Phillip continued to listen to Jason. I knew that Katelyn was probably now also aware that something was very wrong.

"We are on the way," Phillip said abruptly, throwing the phone receiver on the kitchen counter. "Rick has been in an accident. They are air-lifting him to Palmetto Health Regional in Columbia," he said.

Oh God, Oh God, Oh God……I can remember repeating that over and over again, my hands on my head, as I followed Phillip to our bedroom. Forcing myself to focus, I realized he was pulling on his shoes and was trying frantically to think of what to grab before we left the house. Air lifting…helicopter transport…I went suddenly from not being able to breathe to trying to speak in a hyper-calm, collected voice… "Helicopter transport….. We are not coming home tonight. We need to take our contact cases and contact solution."

Katelyn had heard everything. We did not need to tell her that the television show we had been watching minutes ago had just become a horrifying reality in our home. We will probably never watch one of those shows again.

Phillip, Katelyn, and I were probably in the car and headed to Columbia within five minutes of receiving the phone call from Jason. Did we even have enough gas to get there or do we need to stop? Do we have the directions on the GPS to the hospital…what about our other children? Phillip and I discussed briefly whether or not to go ahead and call them. Initially deciding to wait until we got to the hospital and had more information, we quickly changed our minds as we thought about the prevalence of Facebook and Twitter. Also, acknowledging again the apparent gravity of Rick's condition, I knew I needed to call the other children. As Phillip drove, I closed my eyes for just a minute before I began dialing numbers……breath, Terry…..slow, deep breaths……What do you need to tell them? Be calm on the phone… don't panic them. Knowing the closeness of our family, I knew that was highly unlikely.

"Emily, this is Mom."…slow deep breath, Terry…"Rick has been in a car accident. He is being transported to Palmetto Richland Hospital in Columbia." I paused briefly as Emily began firing questions on the other end of the phone. "Dad, Katelyn, and I are on the way to the hospital, Em. We don't know how bad it is. You may not drive yourself. Find someone to drive you to the hospital and meet us there. I love you Em."

Hanging up the phone, I then dialed Phillip Jr.'s number, giving him the same information and instructions. Putting the phone down for a minute, I turned towards the back seat of the car and took Katelyn's hand. "Are you Ok?" I asked her quietly. My heart absolutely broke for this seventeen year old daughter of mine.

I faced the front of the car again, my eyes filling up with tears as I begged Phillip to turn on the emergency flashers and drive faster.

At the age of seventeen, as a senior in high school, I had been through this whole scenario before. All of those memories and emotions suddenly came flooding in and made me feel as though I was suffocating.

We had had a great family weekend, visiting one of my older sisters at Wofford College. It was a beautiful Sunday afternoon in October and we were back at home dressing for a 50th wedding anniversary party that we were scheduled to attend. My dad was a physician, and was called away to the hospital at the last minute, delaying our departure for the party, so I rode on ahead with friends of my parents. The plan was for my mom and dad to come a little later, after he swung by the hospital to check on a patient. They never arrived at the party that afternoon. As they made the thirty minute drive to the party, a car ran a stop sign, killing my dad instantly. My mom died about an hour later. That is how I remember my senior year in high school.

Hiding my face from Katelyn so that she could not see the now steady stream of tears rolling down my cheeks, I began to pray that similar circumstances were not going to be a part of her senior year.

Forcing my mind back into the present, Phillip and I began to talk about Ben, our youngest son. Ben was a freshman at Anderson University and had only been away at school for two weeks. Again acknowledging the strength and closeness of our family, we knew that we had to figure out a way to get Ben to Columbia. Calling my sister, Rebecca, who also lives in the Anderson area, I explained the situation to her. "I will do whatever you need me to," she said. After much discussion with Phillip, Rebecca went to the campus of AU, and she and the security guard went to Ben's dorm room. Phillip talked to Ben on the phone and he quickly gathered some of his things before getting in the car with my sister to make the trip to Columbia. I will always be so grateful to Rebecca for all that she did to love and support all of us during this time of crisis for our family.

The drive to the hospital seemed like an eternity. As we pulled into the emergency area, we could hear the sound of the helicopter. As we looked up, we were able to see the helicopter blades still whirling on the roof-top of the hospital. Everything felt like it was in slow-motion…like it wasn't real. I shuddered as I thought of sitting at home watching TV. I wanted to wake up, realizing that I had somehow fallen asleep on the couch and could go crawl into my nice warm bed beside Phillip. Pulling my jacket around me in the cool night air, I was forced to settle for gripping his hand as we ran towards the emergency room entrance, Katelyn close behind.

After briefly checking in at the front desk, we were immediately taken back to a small waiting room. Like a horse being forced into the entrance of a stall, I realized that Phillip was not going in. As our eyes met, without saying a word, we both stood quietly just outside the small room where they had indicated for us to wait. As a pastor, Phillip had been in rooms like that many times with other families as they had received news about their loved ones. He knew what those rooms were for. He would not go in that room. My heart hurt for him and I felt terrified as I realized what he was thinking.

Phillip Jr. and Emily had arrived. Misty, Rick's girlfriend, was also there with us. We huddled in the hallway, hugging each other and gripping hands as we waited for a report on Rick. We knew, from what Jason had told Phillip on the telephone, that Rick had been in and out of consciousness as they loaded him onto the helicopter for transport, but that's about all that we knew. I was growing desperate for information. All of the emotions of being a mother were colliding with any nursing logic that I typically would have had in similar situations. I would struggle with wearing both of those hats for many weeks to come.

While we were waiting, Marshall Lillard, the highway patrolman who responded to the call (and was also a member of our church) stayed with us. We were slowly able to begin piecing together the events leading up to Rick's accident. He had been at his home group bible study meeting that evening, leaving the meeting around 9:30 p.m. He left the meeting by himself, driving his truck. He had driven a soft-top jeep up until graduating from Clemson several months before the accident, but upon graduation was adamant about getting a truck. I argued with him several times about getting that truck, not wanting him to go into additional debt to purchase it. I am thankful now that he did not listen to me because the size of that truck helped to protect Rick that night. The roads were wet and the highway patrolman said that based on the skid marks, Rick had either hydroplaned or swerved to miss a deer. Veering suddenly to the right, Rick's truck left the road, plowing over several small pine trees, before finally coming to a rest with the truck bed partially submerged in a pond. The front of the truck now sat with its headlights pointing back towards the road. As another car passed, they were able to see the headlights shining from the edge of the pond.

As the highway patrolman continued to talk, and as Phillip talked to Nathan, one of the first responders on the phone, we were getting a clearer picture of what had happened to Rick. By the time the emergency responders were on the scene, Rick was sitting in water up to his hips, confused and asking to be taken to his house. Aware that he was sitting in water, Rick had unbuckled his seat belt but had not been able to get himself out of the belt due to a severe fracture of the left collarbone. The truck was a mangled mess, the roof almost completely caved in by the trees that now lay across the front of the truck. Nathan was able to crawl into the truck through the passenger side window and began to assess Rick's injuries, staying right beside Rick until the other responders were able to extricate Rick from the rubble. Our family is immeasurably thankful to Nathan and to all of the responders on the scene that night.

I had heard all that I could stand to hear. The visual images of our son sitting in that truck as the cool, dark night and water enveloped him were details that I would continually attempt to block from my mind. Feeling fear and panic once again grip me, I struggled to stay composed around our other children. I fought the urge to run screaming from the building. I searched Phillip's face for hope and comfort and watched as he nervously fumbled with the buttons on his shirt. We had talked so many times about my parents' accident, about fears that he had if and when something happened to someone close to him. Phillip is a rock. In our twenty-seven years of marriage and raising five kids, he has and always will be my steady oar. The waters were getting choppy for our entire family, but he would be a steady oar for all of us. I knew that, no matter what.

As we stood out in the hallway, the doctors and nurses were working feverishly on Rick. His vital signs were all stable but he was very confused and combative. As his level of consciousness decreased, the trauma doctors decided to intubate him. Clearing blood and vomit from his mouth they placed a breathing tube in his airway and placed him on a breathing machine. He had obvious severe deformity of the left collar bone area, a deep laceration on his forehead and left elbow, and blood oozing from his left ear. Cutting away his clothes with large trauma scissors, the trauma team continued their initial assessment of Rick, moving from head to toe like a well-oiled machine. Portable x-rays were done confirming a left clavicle fracture, and also ruled out any spinal cord injuries. That is when we finally got our first report on Rick's condition.

"Are you the Lee family?" the doctor asked, barely allowing the door to swing closed behind her before she started talking. "I am one of the trauma doctors working with Preston," she said, scanning all of our faces as she continued in a low, steady voice.

"Rick," I said. "We call him Rick."

"I don't know how much information you have been given. Rick was brought in to the emergency department following a single car accident. He has a fractured left clavicle and some lacerations, but we also believe, because of his altered mental status and blood coming from his ear, that he may have an intracranial hemorrhage. He may be bleeding in his brain. We have put in a breathing tube and we are taking him to the CT scanner to further evaluate the extent of head injury and then will be taking him to the surgical trauma intensive care unit (STICU). There is a waiting room on the fifth floor of the

STICU where all of you can wait. I will let you know as soon as I have more information."

Then she disappeared.

I can barely remember what happened after that. I felt numb, but was also aware of my trembling and tears. I have no idea how or when we all made it up to the fifth floor. My heart ached as I watched Phillip and the other children cry, gripping each other occasionally as we waited. Emily sobbed to the point of vomiting several times. I felt totally helpless in my attempt to console her. Dear God, this is a nightmare. Please wake us up. My whispers of prayer began like never before that night, and "praying without ceasing" took on a whole new meaning. September 4th, 2012 would be a night we would never forget, and a night that Rick Lee would never remember.

Where life veered off course

Brokenhearted

"The Lord is close to the brokenhearted and saves those whose spirits have been crushed."
Psalm 34:18 (NLT)

We sat for several more hours on the fifth floor, anxiously waiting for the doors to the STICU to open and for someone to bring us more information about Rick. The waiting room was beginning to fill with people who had heard of Rick's accident and we were overwhelmed with love and support. Rebecca and Ben had arrived from Anderson and I felt a huge sigh of relief as I saw them both stepping off of the elevator. Finally, one of the trauma physicians emerged and the report that she gave to us regarding Rick's condition was grave.

The CT scan showed subarachnoid hemorrhaging in Rick's brain, explaining his now fully comatose state. A fractured rib had also punctured his left lung, requiring the surgeons to perform an emergency thoracotomy. Making an incision in between two of Rick's ribs, a large flexible tube was inserted through the chest wall and into the pleural space. The chest tube would help to remove the accumulation of air or fluid in that space, allowing Rick's lung to re-inflate. During helicopter transport to the hospital and also during the intubation, (the insertion of the breathing tube), Rick had vomited large amounts of the meal that he had ingested hours before. Aspirating, or inhaling, the fluid and food into the bronchi and lungs, the doctors also had to perform an emergency bronchoscopy on Rick. An instrument was inserted into his airway through the endotracheal tube (breathing tube), and then down into the left and right main stem bronchus and right lower lobe of Rick's lung, where it was noted to be completely blocked off by food material. With the use of saline lavage and suction techniques, and after multiple insertions of the suction tube, most of the food material was removed.

"We will repeat the CT scans on Rick every six hours to re-assess the hemorrhaging in his brain. The next 24-48 hours will be critical for him. You can go in to see him now and we will keep you informed if there are any changes in his condition," the surgeon said, lingering for a moment to answer our flood of questions.

We stood over Rick's bed, brokenhearted and in disbelief. He lay motionless, his chest moving only when the ventilator triggered a breath. Holding his hand, we all took turns talking to him, straining expectantly to feel a hand squeeze back. There was nothing. His face and body were already very swollen and small amounts of blood continued to ooze from his ear.

"How do you go from just driving home from bible study to this?" I cried. No one answered, as we all stood sobbing around Rick's bed.

I felt sick and totally helpless as I watched Phillip and the children survey Rick. It was surreal to see all of the machines surrounding him and tubes attached to him. As ventilator and EKG alarms sounded, I tried to explain some of the equipment to them, hoping it would help. Recognizing their blank stares, I knew that we were all already saturated with information and in sensory over-load. Silence now, against the background buzz of ICU activity, was all that we were able to hear.

We stood around Rick's bed for as long as the ICU staff would allow us to. Before leaving his side, we all held hands, and placing hands on Rick, Phillip prayed the first of many prayers that would serve to unite, comfort, and lead our family in an irreplaceable way. Again, feeling brokenhearted and crushed in spirit, we cried out to God for Rick's healing and for our comfort and peace in the middle of this tragedy. Just as the sun rose over the horizon, we made our way back to the waiting room. We had made it through the first night.

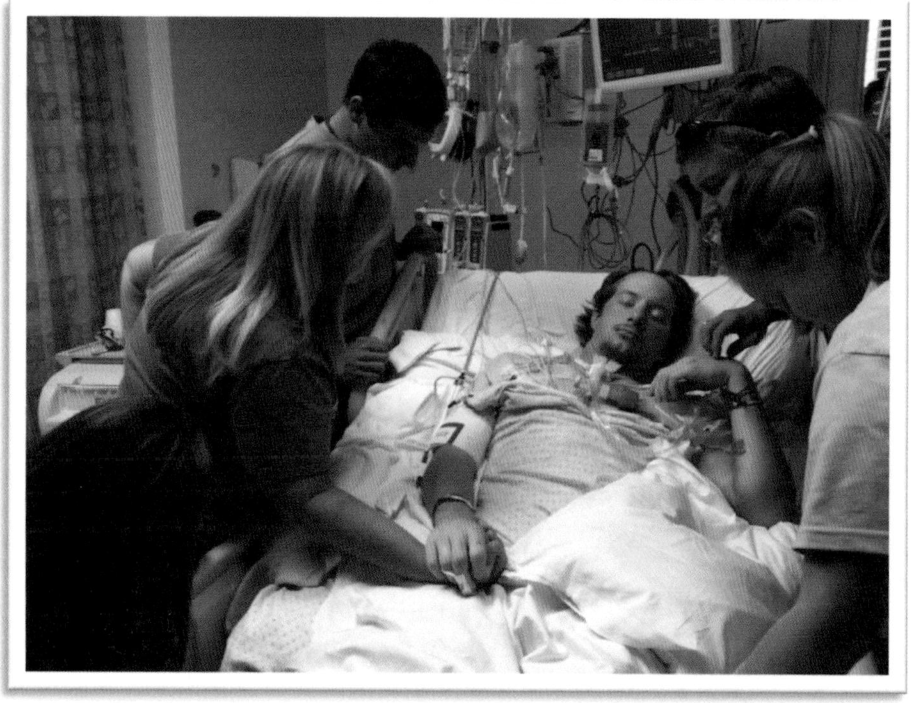

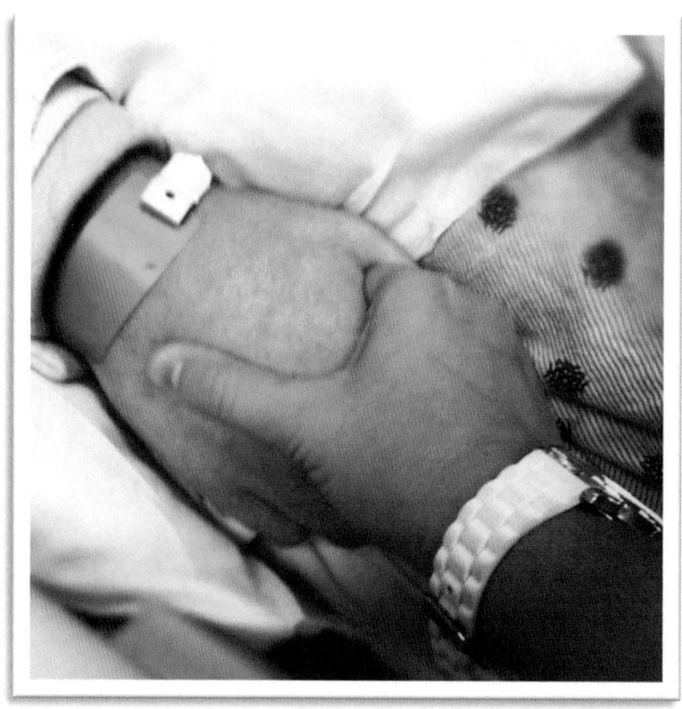

The Slumber

"...how long will you sleep...when will you wake up..."
Proverbs 6:9 (NLT)

"Wake up, Rick! Come on, Buddy, it's time to get up!" Phillip called from the top of the stairs.

That's a scene that is so familiar at our house. Rick loves to sleep! We would always start waking him up well before it was actually time for him to get up. Maybe he is what the Bible describes in Proverbs as a sluggard! "Wake up, Rick!" began to take on a whole different meaning for us.

"Wake up, Rick!" Rick's nurse, Abbey, yelled as she rubbed hard on Rick's sternum with her knuckles. His arms curled just a little…withdrew a little from the painful stimulus…but other than that...nothing.

"Rick, Mom and Dad are here. Come on buddy. Wake up…open those eyes. Come on, Rick!" we yelled.

Nothing.

He continued to lay motionless, still connected to all the machines, tubes coming from everywhere. Minutes ticked into hours as we watched and waited. We watched for the smallest movement…the slightest response to our voice…anything. Anything Rick…… Please show us something so that we know you are still here. Please, Rick.

Nothing.

Abbey was in constant motion around Rick's bed. She was a ball of energy and loved being a nurse. I could tell by the way she cared for Rick. Moving methodically through her morning assessment, she explained everything she was doing. After learning that I was also a nurse, she allowed me to help a little bit with Rick's care. She let me do simple things…like sliding him up in bed to put a pillow under his feet. Things like that were huge to me because it helped me feel as though I were taking care of Rick, too. I loved Abbey for that. I knew that she was taking care of Rick **and** his family. She was a fantastic nurse and became Rick's biggest cheerleader while he was a patient at Palmetto Richland Hospital. We could all sense a very authentic, earnest desire on her part for Rick to wake up, too. Abbey was an angel of mercy and reminded me of so many of the reasons that I became a nurse. Thank you, Abbey. You are a precious gift to everyone that you care for.

Phillip and I stood for long intervals at Rick's bedside, talking to him quietly. The children came in and out, as well as others from Cedar Creek Church that began to fill the STICU waiting room. We also allowed Misty, Rick's girlfriend, to have some private time at Rick's bedside that morning. My heart ached for her as I watched her deal with the reality of what had happened to Rick. I felt overwhelmed many times with the need to care for so many people that were experiencing pain and fear during this ordeal. I found myself "going into nurse mode" when people came in to see Rick, trying to explain all of the machines and tubes that were connected to him. I think that became a coping mechanism for me. If I focused on the medical part for a while, it allowed me to somehow disconnect for a moment from the fact that my son was lying in that bed.

I was brought back to reality when the trauma team doctors entered the room. Rick was in a large intensive care area with three other patients in the room. Curtains separated each patient, but from time to time the curtains were drawn back enough to expose the other trauma patients and their families. As the doctors made rounds from one bed to the next, it was impossible to block out all of the sights and sounds in the room. I wanted to close my eyes and make it all go away. Reaching for the curtain, I pulled it a little more closely around Rick's bed, attempting to wall-off the tidal wave of tragedy that was crashing in all around us. The curtains were not enough to block out the sobs of other family members as they spoke to the doctors. I gripped the side-rail of Rick's bed and searched Phillip's face. He looked as nauseated as I felt.

Finally, it was our turn. The neurosurgeon moved toward us, perched on a little rolling stool. He introduced himself in a very matter-of-fact way and started right in on the details of Rick's injuries.

"He has a severe head injury. The one thing that we know for sure is that we don't know.....We don't know when he will wake up or if he will wake up," he continued, still in an almost nonchalant manner. Maybe I had not heard him correctly.

"What does that mean?' I asked quietly. "I don't understand that. Are there statistics on cases like this? What is realistic for us to hope for?" Phillip and I both leaned in a little towards the doctor as he continued to speak.

"If he doesn't wake up in the first twenty-four hours, then we watch for something during the first week. If he doesn't wake up during the first week after the accident, then the next mile-marker will be within the first year."

And with that, the doctor stood up and left the room. I thought that he had gone to answer the telephone. I thought that maybe he went to get some x-rays for us to look at. He did not return.

"Is he gone?" I asked one of the nurses. "We had more questions. He just got up and left. What the hell was that?" I asked incredulously.

Phillip and I both turned to Rick's bed and just stood there. There was deafening silence.

Twenty-four hours...seven days...a year......noise from the ventilator as it breathed into Rick. Twenty-four hours...seven days...during the first year...there are no words to describe the weight of what we had just been told.

POINTS TO PONDER

- **How has your life veered off course unexpectedly?**

- **What is your initial reaction when faced with a crisis?**

- **Relationships are crucial in moments of crisis. Who could you call for help at 3 a.m.?**

- **The Bible teaches that "God is close to the brokenhearted" Do you think that is true? Why or why not?**

People of Faith

"O Lord, why do you stand so far away? Why do you hide when I am in trouble?"
Psalm 10:1 (NLT)

As we had anticipated, the CT scans on Rick's head were repeated every six hours to monitor the bleeding in his brain. The latest CT report showed "blooming" or extension of the subarachnoid bleeding, as well as a slight shift of Rick's brain to one side. That was not the update we were hoping for.

"We need your permission to insert an intracranial pressure monitor (ICP) into Rick's brain," said one of the residents. "We need to monitor the pressure inside the skull. If the pressure continues to rise, we may need to remove a portion of Rick's skull to allow more room for the brain if additional swelling occurs."

Knowing that there were no other options, I nodded affirmatively at Phillip as he took the pen and paper in his hands. Handing the clip board back to the resident, the doctor quickly disappeared again back behind the double doors that led to the STICU.

Rick's scalp was shaved and prepped with betadine and sterile towels were draped over his head to clear a sterile field. Ten cc's of lidocaine with epinephrine were injected into his scalp and down to the bone as a local anesthetic. Cardiac monitoring, respirations, blood pressure, and oxygen saturation were monitored throughout the procedure and recorded by the STICU staff.

After piercing the scalp to the bone with a scalpel, a manual drill was used to pierce the skull bone. The dura, or covering of the brain, was then pierced with the drill bit. The intracranial bolt was then fit into the prepared skull entry site and screwed securely into place. A catheter was placed just below the bolt into the brain parenchyme (tissue) to monitor the brain pressure readings. Throughout the entire procedure, Rick laid motionless, his chest rising and falling in synchrony with the sound of the ventilator.

After the ICP monitor was in place, we were finally allowed back into Rick's room. Standing there staring at him, looking at the fresh shaved bald spot on his head with the ICP monitor awkwardly protruding from his head, I felt hopeless for the first time. I just felt…hopeless. There was no sign that precious Rick, as we knew him, was in any way with us. That thought was unbearable to me. We all moved in closer to touch him and to talk to him, straining to see even the smallest flicker of response from him.

Nothing.

We walked back to the waiting room and I realized that the sun was sinking below the horizon again. It was hard to believe that we had been at the hospital for almost a full twenty-four hours.

"Phillip, we have got to feed the children and they have got to get some sleep," I said.

A hotel room had generously been provided for our family that was within one or two miles of the hospital. Snacks, pillows and blankets, drinks, and multiple other items had also been brought to the hospital. Cedar Creek Church was overwhelming us with the way that they were reaching out to love and support our family. The waiting room was lined with people that had come to pray with us. Every time the elevator doors opened, we were met with another wave of people who had arrived to express their concern and encouragement. There were several people, however, that completely overwhelmed us with their presence.

Gina Hutto is a beautiful lady, both inside and out. Her daughter, Kaley, suffered a severe head injury several years ago after being thrown from a horse. Kaley did not survive the head injury that she sustained in that accident. Now, here stood Gina, in the same hospital waiting room where she had received the most devastating news a parent can hear, seeking to love and support us. The strength that she showed in coming to see us was something that Phillip and I will never forget.

Laura and Dewayne Deal have a similar story. Their son, Alex, had also been in a car accident several years ago, sustaining yet another severe head injury. Alex had recovered after a long and arduous period of rehabilitation. The Deal's willingness to come to the hospital that night is also something that gave us strength and hope at a time when we had little of either.

And finally, Nathan…How do I even begin to describe what I felt when I met Nathan and his wife in the waiting room? Nathan was the EMS first responder on the scene of Rick's accident. Unable to get Rick out of the truck, Nathan climbed in through the passenger side window and stayed beside Rick until they were able to extricate him from the wreckage. But that is only the tip of the iceberg. Nathan was the first responder on the scene of his own daughter's ATV accident…an accident where his daughter had sustained a severe head injury and was taken to Palmetto Richland Hospital. Nathan's daughter died. And now, here he and his wife sat, in the waiting room with us for the first time since that accident.

I have never seen God's strength, manifested in the lives of those individuals, like we did that night. Their strength gave us strength, hope, and courage to face the next moment of our ordeal with Rick. We will forever be grateful to them for allowing God to use them in such a powerful way.

After nearly 28 years of marriage, Phillip knew not to even try to take me away from the hospital that night. As he and the children got on the elevator to head over to the hotel, I turned and realized that Misty was still there. I knew better than to pry her away, too! We laughed a little and cried a lot that night in the hospital together. Instructed to go to the second floor waiting area, we found a space just outside one of the bathrooms where we could lay on the floor to rest for a while. Morning seemed to come before we even closed our eyes. Gathering our things from the floor, we headed back to the STICU.

Please, dear God, please let there be some improvement……PLEASE.

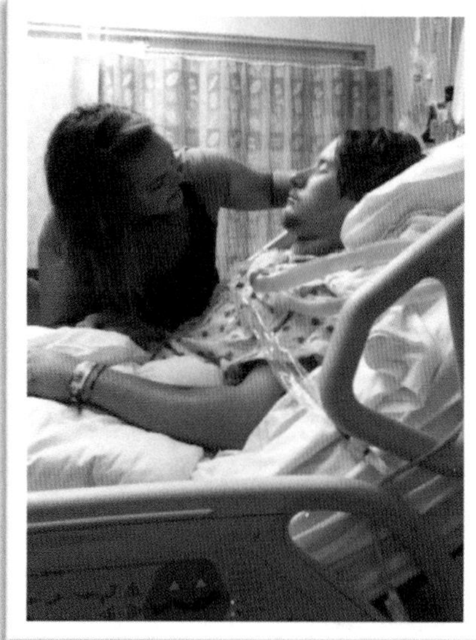

Misty keeping watch

The Aiken community unites in prayer for Rick

Thumbs Up

"Let me hear of your unfailing love each morning, for I am trusting you."
Psalm 143:8

The STICU was a buzz of activity that morning. There had been another multiple car accident on I-20 the night before and the trauma teams had been inundated with patients. There was also a new patient in the bed next to Rick. He was a fairly young man who had sustained a severe head injury while climbing on a ropes course. The activity and number of people around his bed that morning led me to believe his condition was very serious as well.

Rick looked peaceful, but lifeless, as Misty and I arrived at his bedside. Abby reported that he had had a stable night and that there was basically no change in his condition. My eyes scanned the monitors and ventilator, quickly doing my own nursing assessment on my son. Rick's left shoulder was markedly swollen and bruised now from the broken clavicle. The obvious deformity from the break made it painful to even look at. I ran my hand across Rick's forehead, brushing away a few strands of his red hair. Leaning over his side rail, Misty and I spoke softly to Rick from both sides of the bed.

"Rick, Mom is here. Open your eyes. Come on, Rick. It's time to wake up," I whispered.

'Rick, I'm here," Misty said quietly, leaning over to kiss him gently on the cheek.

Straining to see even the smallest response from Rick, there was nothing. Abbey was moving methodically through her morning routine, checking everything on Rick from head to toe. Performing the neurological check, I found a little hope in the fact that Rick's pupils were equal and reactive to light and that he was still responding to painful stimuli. Rick's intracranial pressure had also stayed within normal limits during the night so I was satisfied that we were at least status quo at the moment.

Phillip, Rebecca and the kids came back at some point that morning. I was thankful to see that they looked fairly rested and they were also eager to see Rick and get updates on his condition. It gave me a sense of calm for all of us to be there together. It has always given me a sense of joy and peace to have "all of my chickens in the same coop."

We all spent time around Rick's bed that morning and then continued to sit and talk with folks from Cedar Creek that stopped by to offer us words of encouragement. As we interacted with friends and family, I was amazed to watch Phillip in a pastor role as he visited with other families in the waiting room. He was kind and caring. If I had not known of our own situation with Rick, I am not sure that I would have been able to tell that he was in his own time of crisis with a family member. Just as "going into nurse mode" became a coping mechanism for me, I knew that Phillip connecting and caring for all of those other people was allowing him to cope with and manage his own fear and pain. I was so proud of his strength and sincerity as he moved from one family to the next. We quickly began to share the food and drinks that had been left for our family and we also began to smile and cry with folks as they received updates on their loved ones.

Around mid-day, one of the doctors came out to give us a report on Rick. Asking all of us to go into a small family room, our family sat and listened carefully to Dr. Catherine Loflin. She was a third-year resident and was fantastic with the way that she spoke to us. Her voice was slow and steady. She was very factual and straight to the point, yet was very compassionate and caring at the same time.

"Rick is in respiratory failure. The food and liquid that he inhaled the night of the accident has injured the lining of the lungs, similar to a chemical burn. In addition to the left lung collapse, there is also an area of collapse on the right side. We need to place a second chest tube, now on the right side, to allow that lung to re-inflate." She paused briefly, waiting and watching for us to respond. We were all silent.

"I also want to talk to you about switching Rick from the oral endotracheal tube to a tracheostomy. The tube that we have in his mouth is a tube that we would use for short term management of Rick's breathing. We anticipate that Rick will need longer- term breathing support. We want to make an incision in his neck and place the trach tube there to allow us better management and fewer complications as we continue to treat his respiratory status. We also need to think about Rick's nutritional status. He is not able to eat or drink and the intravenous fluids that we are giving him are not enough. We need to insert a tube, called a PEG tube, into Rick's stomach that will allow us to begin feeding him with calorie-dense liquid nutrition." she explained.

We all sat quietly for a minute, dazed by all of the information. A PEG tube...a trach.....my mind was racing. The only patients I had ever cared for with those tubes were long-term care patients...patients that didn't get better.

"Are you saying that you don't think Rick is going to get better?" I asked in a whisper, aware of my heart pounding in my throat.

"Again, we don't know. It is impossible for us to know with severe head injuries. What we do know is that these two procedures will help us manage his care better." Dr. Loflin said, as she passed the permits to Phillip to be signed.

The children were crying now. Phillip and I remained stoic through the entire conversation, simply trying to digest all of the information. As Dr. Loflin left the room, I went into nurse mode again, asking Phillip and the children if they had understood everything that the doctor had said. The details and plans to manage him better did not feel better to us. It felt much worse. There was an ominous feeling in the room and I knew that I could not explain that part away. The grief and pain that we were feeling could only be treated by Rick waking up.

With nothing else to say, we all got up and left the family room. Numb and exhausted in every way, we scattered for a little while, each to deal with their innermost thoughts of what we had just been told. Phillip went to a remote hallway far away from any activity, laid down with his face to the floor, and sobbed uncontrollably.

I paced back and forth along several corridors of the hospital, now shaking my fist and gritting my teeth in anger. I had been having conversations with God for several months leading up to the accident. I had asked God to reveal to me what "my next" was going to be now that all of my kids were soon to be out of the house. This? Really God, are you kidding me? THIS IS NOT "MY NEXT"! PLEASE GOD! I DON'T WANT THIS TO BE MY NEXT!

Visions of our being Rick's long-term caregivers raced through my mind…doing his tube feedings, suctioning his trach…turning him every two hours so that he would not get bed sores. I remembered Rick walking so proudly through the graduation ceremony at Clemson. I could close my eyes and see him heading out the door to go duck hunting. I could hear him saying, "I am not going to the dentist" when I told him, at the age of twenty-two, that it was time for his dental check-up. My fist pounded the windowsill as tears began to stream down my face. God, take him, I thought. Just take him home now. Please don't leave him like this! I felt total, utter despair and hopelessness. I don't want him to be like this, I thought….but I cannot bear to lose him either. My family will never be the same again. Dear God, why am I going through this again?? What did I not learn the first time?!! Help me, God! Where are you?!

I stood there for quite a while, looking out of the window and gazing up at the puffy clouds that hung over the roof-line. I'm praying, God. I am begging you. Do you even hear me? Do you even know that we are here? I don't feel you right now. I feel afraid and angry. I feel nauseated and exhausted. I don't even feel like praying anymore, I thought, dropping my head and allowing my body to slump against the wall.

We continued to go in and out of Rick's room all afternoon. The children were also having a horribly difficult day. Hoping and praying that good news would come from the doctor's update, we now felt even more discouraged and distraught. We all needed something.....anything......the smallest little thing to tell us that Rick was still with us and that there was still hope.

Phillip and the kids were visiting with folks out in the waiting room so I decided to go back to see Rick one more time before Abbey went home for the day. It was almost seven o'clock in the evening now and I was beginning to feel a little sick. I knew I probably needed to leave the hospital for a little while just to get a mental and emotional break, but I was not sure how to peel myself away.

As I entered Rick's room, Abbey was doing the hourly neurological check. I watched intently as she did her assessment and she nodded for me to come closer, asking me to stimulate Rick a little bit by talking to him. I leaned over the side rail of Rick's bed and began talking, squeezing his hand at the same time.

"Rick, Mom is here. Rick, open your eyes. Come on, Rick…you sleep all the time! Wake up, Rick!"

"Rick," Abbey said. "Come on Rick, give me a 'thumbs up', Rick" she said, pulling on his right hand. "Rick!" Abbey yelled, leaning in a little closer. "I want to see a 'thumbs up'… …..come on!"

One more time, Abbey yelled into Rick's ear, and all of a sudden, there was the slightest movement in Rick's right thumb. Abbey and I gasped at the same time, looking cautiously at each other, almost afraid to believe what we had just seen. Now Abbey got a little more insistent with Rick, coaxing him once more to give a big "thumbs up" as she rubbed hard on his chest with her knuckles. Rick withdrew both arms slightly as she rubbed on his chest. He finally gave a very definitive "thumbs up" gesture with his right thumb.

"He did it, Abbey!!" I hollered. "That was a 'thumbs up'!!! Oh, my gosh! I saw it!" I exclaimed. Abbey and I both cried and hugged each other for a moment, both of us aware of the fact that we had just seen the first purposeful movement from Rick since the night of the accident. Running towards the waiting room, I barged through the doors and screamed, "Rick gave a 'thumbs up'!!! He heard us!!! We know he did!!!"

And with that, we had what we needed for the moment. We had a glimmer of hope.

Phillip and Abbey

Waiting and Wondering

"Lord you alone are my inheritance, my cup of blessing. You guard all that is mine."
Psalm 16:5 (NLT)

We all slept better that night. Leaving a precious friend in the waiting room, and our phone numbers with the nursing staff, it felt strange to leave the hospital but seemed the wisest thing to do. We all needed a break and some rest before Rick's surgery the next day.

Sitting on the beds in the hotel, we all talked for a little while before going to sleep. Phillip and I both knew that the kids were being inundated with so much information and that they were all dealing with a wide variety of emotions. We knew that we needed to be intentional about encouraging them to vent how they were feeling and give them the opportunity to ask questions. I was amazed by all of them. Phillip, Emily, Katelyn, and Ben were all showing huge maturity and strength. We circled up, help hands, and prayed for Rick and each other before crashing for the night.

Talking Philip and the kids into sleeping in the next morning, I got up early and headed back to the hospital around 5:30am for the first visiting hour. Arriving on the fifth floor, I stood just outside the double doors that led to the STICU and rang the nurse's station.

"May I come back to room 527 to visit please?" I asked, as the secretary answered the phone.

"It's going to be a little while," she answered. "The nurses are busy right now."

Disappointed, I sat reluctantly in one of the waiting room chairs closest to the doors. I reasoned that the nurses were in the middle of bathing the patients and doing last minute shift stuff. I had worked many night shifts in the ICU and I knew how busy and behind the nurses could get, especially if they had multiple patients. I sat for an hour or so, watching the clock and flipping nervously through a magazine. I wanted to see Rick and waiting had never been one of my strong points. Walking up to the telephone again, I called back to the nurse's station a second time.

"May I come back to room 527 now?" I asked, trying to hide my impatience.

"Wait just a minute. Let me check." Pause... Pause...Pause... "No, the nurses are busy in the room. It's going to be a little longer."

Hanging the phone back on the receiver, I paced back and forth, trying to decide what to do. Thinking about the three other patients in Rick's room and the severity of their injuries, I sat back down and decided it was a realistic scenario. Stop worrying, I said to myself.

Minutes ticked away and I must have dozed off at some point. Opening my eyes and glancing at the clock, I realized that it was almost eight o'clock. Shift change had occurred and surely the morning rush was over now. I picked up the phone for the third time and waited for someone to answer.

"I am coming in to room 527," I announced this time, stating my intention rather than asking permission. Again, the voice on the other end said that I could not come in.

"Ok, I understand what you are saying. I am Rick Lee's mom and you need to tell me now if something is wrong with Rick. Is that the patient that they have been busy with all morning? I want to know what is wrong. NOW!" I said emphatically. "I am not waiting any longer!" I was now completely convinced that there was something that they were not telling me.

"I will try to get a report to you on your son," said the secretary. "Give me just a minute."

Within a matter of minutes, the double doors opened and one of the ICU nurses came out. Sitting in the chair beside me, she began to explain what had happened. “Rick started coughing and his ventilator alarms started to sound. I decided to suction him to get all of the secretions out of his tube so that he could breathe better. As I was suctioning him, he bit down on his breathing tube. He bit down on the tube so hard that he bit a hole completely through the tube. With a hole in the tube, we were not able to keep his oxygen levels up, so the tube was emergently removed and replaced by a new tube. It has taken us a while to get him settled down and stabilized again. I am sorry that you had to wait,” finished the nurse. She seemed very sincere and I could tell that what she had just described had been an ordeal for her.

“Can I go back to see him now?” I asked, nodding my head to indicate that I had understood what she had told me.

Motioning for me to come on back, we walked down that hall together. Arriving at his bedside, we each stood looking at Rick.

“He looks pretty peaceful now, doesn’t he?” said the nurse shaking her head and smiling towards Rick. I knew that the nurse was probably glad that she was heading home!

By now, Phillip and the kids had arrived at the hospital for the day. Filling them in on the events of the morning, we all gathered around Rick’s bed. Hoping to see another “thumbs up” from Rick, we watched as the new nurse performed his neurological check.

Unable to get any response, we all retreated back to the waiting room while the nurse finished doing Rick’s morning care. Knowing that he had to be sedated earlier in the morning, we were hoping that we would be able to see a response later.

Rick was taken to surgery between three and four o’clock that afternoon for his trach and peg tube insertion. The surgery went well and we were thankful to see him after the procedures were completed. With the oral endotracheal tube removed, we were able to see Rick’s entire face and that made a huge difference. The ventilator tube was now connected to the trach in Rick's neck and he seemed to be resting quietly. The anesthesia and medication that they had given him for pain during the surgery would take several hours to wear off. We were once again at the end of another long day and we left the hospital asking God to watch over and protect Rick through another night.

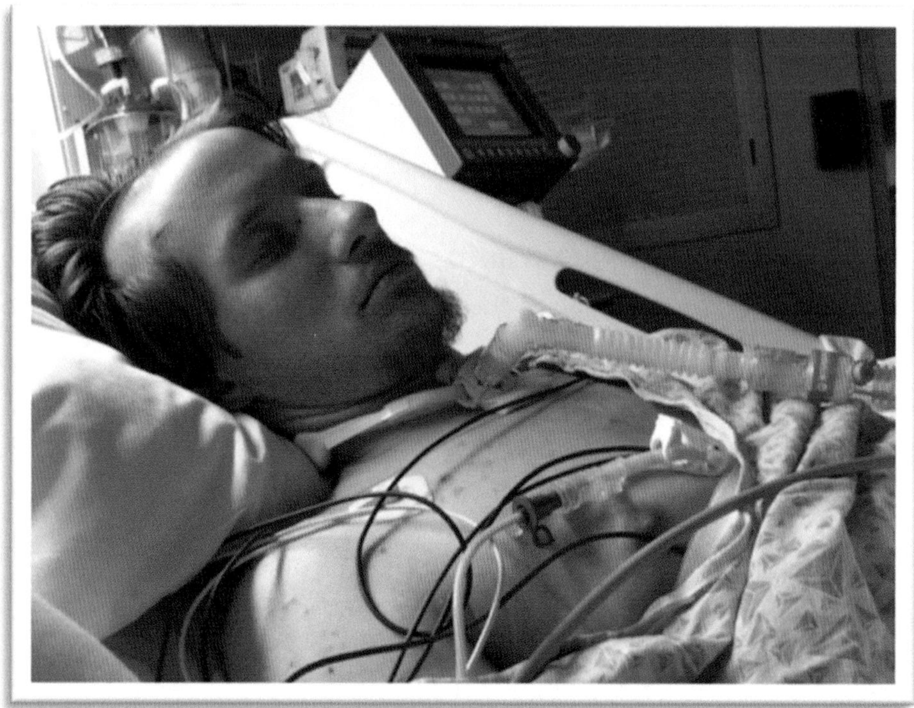

Resting after Trach and PEG Tube Surgery

POINTS TO PONDER

- **In Psalms 10, David feels abandoned by God. How is that possible if God is closest in times of trouble?**

- **Are there certain types of circumstances in life that cause you to question God's love and presence?**

- **Has there ever been a time that you have had to wait for something to happen? What is it about waiting that makes it difficult for you?**

Depths of Despair

"Cast all your cares upon Him: for He cares for you."
1 Peter 5:7

Her name is Ms. Ruby and we are pretty sure that she is an angel. Phillip and I met her the next morning. Arriving at the hospital very early, we decided to go spend some time in the chapel before going up to the STICU area.

As we entered the chapel, we found an elderly lady dressed in a hospital cleaning staff uniform. Her Bible was open on the table in front of her. We apologized for interrupting, but she insisted we come in and sit down. She told us that she started every day by praying and reading her Bible in the chapel. We did not respond. Sitting on one of the benches, we stared quietly at a cross that was hanging on the wall.

Ms. Ruby closed her Bible and went over to a small prayer bench in the corner. Kneeling down on the bench, Ms. Ruby began her prayer time. Ms. Ruby worshipped. There was no band, no stage and no music…just a grateful heart crying out to God for His presence and His strength…"for these old limbs as I work today." And then she asked God to be with this couple that had just come in. We could tell she wasn't saying it for our benefit. She was just talking to Jesus like He was the only one in the room. She stood, and as she slowly made her way to the door, she turned to us and said, "I lost my only son in 2000, and He is faithful no matter what happens. God will give you all you need." And with that, the door opened and she left. But as she went down that hall, we could hear her saying over and over again the name of Jesus…Jesus…Jesus…. until finally we sat in silence again in the chapel. Nothing else needed to be said.

We were so anxious to see Rick that morning. Hopeful that all of the medication had worn off, we went in fully expecting to see Rick responding with a "thumbs up" as soon as we stimulated him. But much to our dismay, there was nothing. He still pulled his arms back a little when we pressed on his sternum, but there was no thumbs up…there was no hand squeezing …his eyes were not open at all. There was still no response at all. Why?? Why was he still not waking up?? But the next thing that we saw was even more baffling. The patient that was in the bed next to Rick was sitting on the side of the bed. This patient had come in after Rick, also with a serious head injury, and had also been in a coma for several days. Now this patient was awake, sitting, and then minutes later, with the help of several physical therapists, came walking slowly past Rick's bed. We were overjoyed for the patient and for his family. But my joy for them soon disappeared and was replaced again by fear and anger as I looked back at the still motionless body of my son. Tears stung my eyes and I finally gave way to quiet sobs as I grasped Rick's hand in mine. Why wasn't Rick waking up? He's been in here even longer than that patient! I can't believe that patient is walking! Oh God, I am so thankful for them. But God, I AM MAD! I WANT RICK TO WAKE UP TOO! I WANT RICK TO WALK! I could not stifle the sobs any longer. I buried my head in one of Rick's pillows and my grief and anger exploded. Drawing the curtains around Rick's bed, the nurse stood there quietly with her hand on my shoulder.

"Why?" I asked her, looking from her to Rick. "Why is he not waking up?"

"We don't know," she said quietly. "I am sorry. Is there anything that I can get for you?"

"No, I just need Rick to wake up." I responded. I tried not to listen as the nurses made preparations for the other patient to be transported out of ICU to a regular room. My heart ached and I closed my eyes for a minute, leaning my head on the side rail of Rick's bed. I felt a pain that I knew I could not medicate away. There was no substance in the whole world that I could have taken to lessen the grief that I was feeling at that moment. I felt so ashamed of my resentment and anger towards the other patient, even towards Phillip as he hugged the neck of the wife and other family members. I did not want a pastor or anybody else near me. I did not want anybody to touch me. I drew away from the nurse and walked over to the other side of the bed to stand and gaze at Rick, still lying lifeless in the bed.

We took the children back to the chapel that afternoon to sit and talk for a little while. We had all hit a very low point and admitted to one another that we were losing hope…we were all beginning to feel like Rick was not going to wake up.

"I want my brother back," sobbed Philip Jr., his shoulders heaving as he continued to cry. He talked about time having slipped away over the past several years and about all the opportunities that he and Rick had had to spend time together. He was now weighed down by the regret of those missed opportunities.

"I am afraid that if Rick wakes up he won't be able to remember all the stuff we have done together," cried Emily. "What if he can't remember anything at all?" No one had any answers.

"I don't understand what a coma is. Why won't he just wake up? What's keeping him from opening his eyes? Can he hear us when we talk to him?" Katelyn asked, wiping the tears away as they left a small trail on her cheeks. I tried to answer her questions but I could tell that I had not been very successful.

Ben sat quietly taking it all in. I knew that he had a wealth of wisdom and emotion lying beneath the surface, but I also knew that he needed time to process everything that was happening. I had learned over the years that Ben will talk when Ben is ready to talk. He has always been wise beyond his years and is one of the most gentle and caring people I have ever known.

We all cried, expressing fear, anger, hopelessness, doubt, and exhaustion. Phillip said he felt like two sides of a coin, full of faith on one side, yet weak and afraid on the other. He'd been tossed in the air and was not sure which side he'd land on. But once again, I saw the truest, most evident calling of pastor on my husband's life as he instructed us to circle up to pray. During that prayer time, all alone in the chapel that afternoon, we cast all of our cares on Jesus. We were totally open, honest and transparent before God. We did not look like or sound like what most people would probably expect from a pastor's family that day. But we knew that God was there and that He loved us and accepted us just the way we were. That was the one thing that we were sure of.

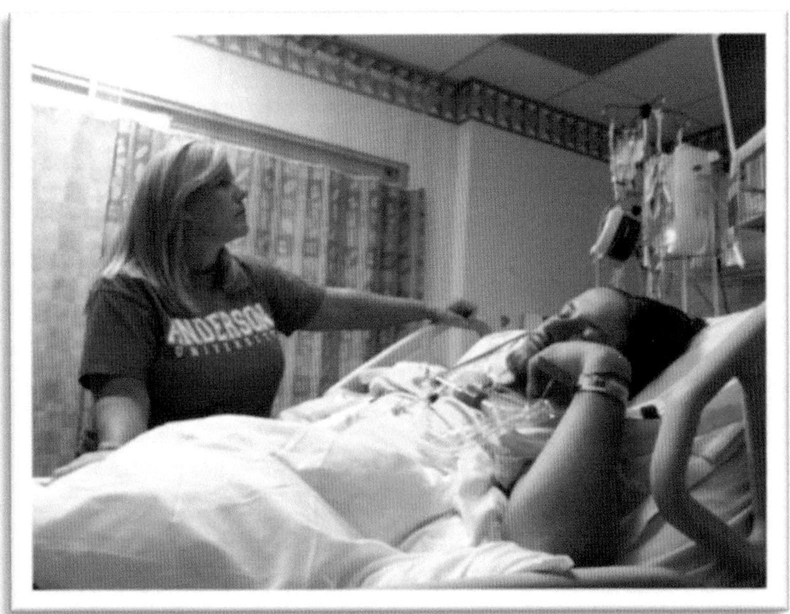

Impossible to separate the mother and the nurse

The Power of Prayer

"'What do you mean, if I can?' Jesus asked. 'Anything is possible if a person believes.' The father instantly cried out, 'I do believe but help me overcome my unbelief.'"
Mark 9:23-24

It was Sunday morning and we were all continuing to struggle with unbelief. We all got up early to head back to the hospital. Phillip and I had just started talking about what to do with the other children's schedules. They had already missed almost a full week of work and/or school and we knew that we had to make decisions regarding their continuing to stay at the hospital every day…"Twenty four hours…seven days… …sometime during the first year"…that continued to ring constantly through our minds as we thought about the other children.

We were especially concerned about Ben. He had only been at Anderson University for two weeks before the accident and was still very much settling into the freshman routine. It still amazes me how God supplies just the right people in our lives to speak wisdom and bring clarity when we need it the most.

Phillip and I were sitting in the hospital, trying to decide what to do with the kids. Luke Pruitt, our pediatrician when we lived in Columbia, just "happened" to come walking by, on his way to STICU to check on us. Seeing us sitting in the lobby, he came over to speak with us.

"Luke, help us decide what we need to do about the other kids," Phillip said. "How long do we let them stay up here?" Quietly, and without hesitation, Luke responded.

"They need to go back to normal as soon as possible. They need to go on back to school."

Probing him a little more, I reminded him that we had just gotten Ben settled at Anderson University and that we were concerned that Ben may not be connected with many friends. Again, Luke did not hesitate with his recommendation. He had such a gentle, yet confident and definitive way of speaking to us. I was so thankful for Dr. Pruitt that day.

Being like-minded and confident that Luke had spoken truth and wisdom to us, Phillip and I went up to the STICU waiting area to talk with the children. They were very resistant to the plan of their leaving the hospital later that day, but we did not make it optional for them. My sister, Rebecca, had been a rock for me all week. She sat at the hospital for hours and hours every day and would then go back to the hotel with us at night. She offered to take Ben back to Anderson later that day and we were so grateful to her for being so available and willing to care for all of us. She was precious to me that week at the hospital and we shed many tears together standing over Rick's bed. I knew that she was hurting, too.

Still feeling discouragement and doubt from the previous day, we all took turns going in to see Rick. He was still not awake, but would occasionally give a weak "thumbs up" when the nurses stimulated him with a sternal rub. He was also moving his right leg around a little bit. I did not see much, if any, activity on the left side and began asking the doctors and nurses about that as they came to his bedside that morning.

"We still do not know why he's not waking up. He does show movement on the right side, but very little on the left. We are suspicious that the bleeding in his brain may have caused a stroke and that may be the reason for what we are seeing. We want to schedule an MRI of his brain but we need to wait until we can decrease his ventilator settings to do the MRI. His lungs are still too sick to be able to take him down for the MRI. We will just have to continue to wait," the neurosurgeon said. He was quickly becoming my least favorite person in the whole wide world!

Holding on to the glimmer of hope that we felt from seeing a "thumbs up", we all went back to the waiting room for a while. I knew that the children were going to need to leave soon and that the departure and separation from us and from Rick's bedside was going to be very difficult. They were already pleading not to leave. The waiting room was almost empty, except for our family. As we sat in the waiting room together, our cell phones started beeping and buzzing with text messages and picture messages coming through on every one. From every single Cedar Creek Church campus, we were getting pictures from throngs of people, praying together and giving a "thumbs up" for Rick. Wc fclt their strength, faith, and belief for healing. When we were in the deepest part of our unbelief, the people of CCC believed for us. The pictures and texts with prayers continued to come all afternoon and those prayers strengthened us and carried us that day in immeasurable ways. Phillip and I grasped hands and caught each other's gaze for a moment. I knew what we were both thinking. We were beginning to believe again.

Later that afternoon, after one final visit with Rick, Rebecca and all the children left. Phillip and I were so proud of all of them. They all showed huge courage and strength that day as they left the hospital, still uncertain of Rick's recovery. It was yet another testimony of God's strength in our weakness. They were an unbelievable blessing to us and to each other as they loved and supported one another.

Leaving a few friends in the waiting room, Phillip and I left the hospital briefly to grab a bite to eat with a few other friends. Driving about two miles away, we had just gotten our food when the phone rang.

"Terry, this is Tonia. One of the nurses just came out and wants to talk with ya'll."

"We are on the way," I said, chunking up the rest of my food and jumping up from my seat.

"Drive faster!" I said to Phillip, as he drove down the road. "Will you just let me out at the front door while you park the car?" I said nervously. I did not know whether to be scared or excited. A million possibilities were racing through my head. "Oh I wish we had never left the hospital," I thought.

Driving up to the front of the hospital, I opened the car door and jumped out before the car stopped rolling. Sprinting to the hospital elevators as quickly as my short, pudgy legs would allow, I rode up to the fifth floor and sprang off of the elevator. Glancing up at the clock, I realized it was seven o'clock, time for change of shift. Oh no, I thought, they aren't going to let me in.

I turned and reached for the phone to call back to the nurses' station. A lady dressed in a uniform saw me and opened the door to the STICU, allowing me to enter. I believe to this day that she was another Ms. Ruby.

Reaching Rick's room, I paused for a moment at the door. The curtain was partially drawn around his bed. I could see his feet and could also see several nurses standing around Rick's bed. I held my breath for a moment, not sure of what to do and afraid of what I was walking in to. As I paused, one of the nurses caught my eye and motioned for me to come in. I eased past the curtain, and there was Rick, sitting up in bed, one eye wide open and one eye still partially closed.

"We thought you might want to see this!" one of the nurses said, smiling from ear to ear.

"Ya' think!?" I said, as we all laughed and hugged briefly.

The room grew quiet as I slid in beside Rick's bed. As I leaned over Rick's side rail, he turned his head to look at me in his "Rick-ish" matter-of-fact way.

"Rick, this is Mom," I said. "If you can hear me, stick out your tongue." Without hesitation, Rick shot up his middle finger!! I laughed hysterically and I am sure all the nurses thought that I was crazy. It was a huge inside joke between a mother and her son!

"I love you, Rick," I whispered through my tears, squeezing his hand.

"I love you too," Rick mouthed. And with that, he closed his eyes and seemed very peaceful.

Running back to the waiting room, I exploded through the doors screaming, "Rick woke up! Rick woke up!! Rick woke up!!!"

So that ended a day in the life of our family and Cedar Creek Church. After a day of typical, authentic, wide-open CCC worship and the prayers of thousands of people … and while God had the attention of all of those people…RICK LEE WOKE UP!

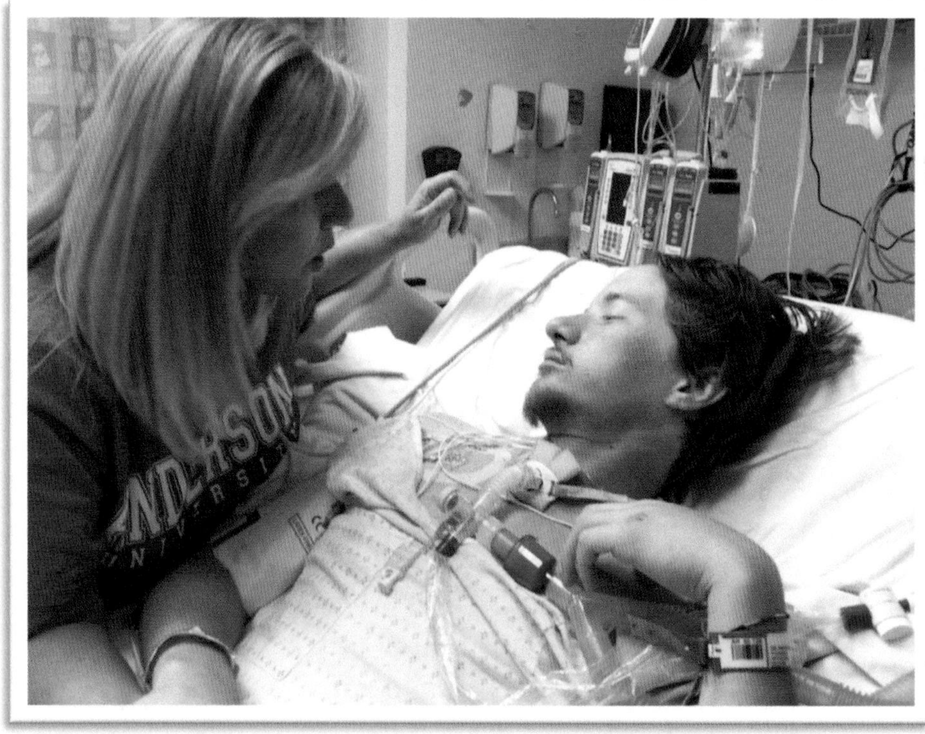

One eye open, one eye closed…but he's awake!

Little Lessons

"I will be filled with joy because of you. I will sing praises to your name, oh most high"
Psalm 9:1 (NLT)

Phillip and I could barely sleep that night. We were exhausted, but felt like we could have run a marathon. We talked for a while before going to sleep. It was so hard to describe all of the emotions that we were feeling as we spent day after day in the ICU waiting room. We left the hospital that day overjoyed that Rick had woken up, yet we also knew that other families were leaving to start planning a funeral. I asked Phillip questions about miracles and about how God answers prayer, wondering about the mystery of it all.

"I wish that I could give you answers to those questions, but I can't," he said quietly. "I don't understand why God works the way He does, but I have come to this conclusion....we have a choice. We can choose to trust God only when life makes sense and when things are going our way or we can choose to trust Him no matter what happens. I guess that's what real faith is all about. I am just praying that God will help me be a man of real faith. I guess the bottom line is this....the same God who is healing Rick is also lovingly carrying those other families through their pain and loss. His love and faithfulness are not measured by our circumstances or by our ability to understand everything. It is based on His character and His promise that when we trust Him, He will make all things work together for His glory and for our good, not just in the short term, but in light of eternity."

I lay awake for a long time after Phillip had drifted off to sleep. I began to go over the past six days in my mind, thinking about all that we had been through and all that we had seen God do in our midst. My mind also drifted back to that Sunday afternoon when my parents' lives had ended so suddenly.... now fast forwarding to this Sunday afternoon when my son had woken from a coma to utter the words "I love you." I will pray to be a woman of faith, I thought, nestling up against the warmth and security that Phillip was providing.

I felt so thankful for all of the people that had loved and encouraged us over the past week. I remembered a conversation I had with Gail Gingrey on the first evening after Rick's accident. Gail had been like a mother to me since our family moved to Aiken. We have never spent much time together, but after every encounter with Gail, I have always felt very nurtured and cared for. Standing in the middle of a throng of people in the hospital waiting room, Gail had quietly taken my hands in hers and said in a very gentle voice, "Rick is going to be OK, Terry. I just feel it," she said. Leaning back a little so I could look into Gail's face, I felt an overwhelming sense of peace and calm in what she was saying. I will admit that I did not believe what she was saying at the time, but I held on to what she spoke to me that evening at the hospital. I was so appreciative for Gail's "mothering" me that night.

I also thought about so many other folks that had cared for us...Butch...Wes... Dean...Beau...the hours in the waiting room with Renee and Tonia...my nursing confidants Gail Hendrix and Anita. And I remembered the desperate phone calls to my twin brother and my friend, Amy. We were blessed beyond measure to have so many people caring for us.

Waking early the next morning, we headed back to the hospital, finally feeling a little bit refreshed. We were anxious to see Rick and see how he was continuing to respond since he had woken up. We were so excited to see his eyes open as we walked into the room. One eye was still very sluggish, but he was definitely awake and following commands. There was still little movement on the left side and when Rick grimaced in pain there was markedly more movement on the right side of his face than on the left. I wondered if Rick was guarding the movement of his left arm because of the pain of his broken clavicle, but why was he not moving his left leg? Desperately trying to stay focused on the huge positive of Rick waking up, I could feel my nursing mind beginning to question deficits that I could see in Rick. It was obvious that Rick was in severe pain when he did attempt to move around, so we tried to quiet him a little after the nurses left his bedside. Even though Rick was able to follow simple commands, it was impossible to assess how oriented he was to the surroundings. When he opened his eyes at intervals, Phillip would lean in and quietly whisper in his ear. "Rick, you've been in an accident. You wrecked your truck. You are in the hospital," assured Phillip.

The nurses gave us a report on the plans for Rick's day. They were hoping to possibly take Rick down some time that afternoon to do the MRI on Rick's brain, continuing to be concerned about a possible stroke. We were so thankful that Rick had woken up, but we knew that we were still definitely not out of the woods.

Leaving Phillip with Rick for a while, I wandered down the hallway to a quiet place where I could call and check on the rest of the children. Gail Gingrey had a niece that also attended Anderson University, so Gail had called ahead to let her niece know that Ben had returned to campus. Upon his arrival, Ben was met by a small entourage of young ladies. Ben was being well cared for!

As I finished with my calls, I turned to head back to the STICU, realizing that Rick's neurosurgeon was headed down the hall. "Rick woke up!!" I said to him excitedly. We had not seen this particular doctor for a day or two. Never hesitating or breaking his gait, he nodded at me ever so slightly and continued down the hallway, his hands jammed in his pockets. If I had a stick, I would have beat him like pancake batter!

"He needs a vacation or a new profession!" I told Phillip as we were talking about the encounter later.

I have thought about that particular physician many times since Rick's accident and my attitude has softened somewhat regarding him. I cannot imagine doing what he does day in and day out. He is faced with an endless stream of tragedy. Some get better, but many do not recover. He faces grieving families day after day that are seeking answers to questions that he does not have. My prayer now is that this physician will be comforted and strengthened by the One and Only Great Physician.

We waited all day for Rick to go down for the MRI and finally, late that afternoon, they were able to decrease the ventilator settings to an appropriate level to transport him to the x-ray department. Another long day was drawing to a close and Phillip and I prepared to leave the hospital again to get some rest. We had already been told that the MRI results would not be available until the next day, so we decided to leave Rick to sleep after the test was completed.

` Driving to Phillip's brother's house about twenty minutes away, we decided to run by Wal-Mart to pick up a few things. It was late and we were both weary. Standing in the check-out aisle, I could only imagine what I must have looked like. My clothes were wrinkled and my hair was pulled back in a pony-tail. Phillip fumbled through his wallet, staring off in the distance a time or two, not even hearing what the check-out attendant was saying. How many times have we stood in the check-out isle, aggravated at people because they were slowing us down? Zoned out? I realized all of a sudden that we were learning so many things in the midst of this ordeal with Rick. Instead of being impatient with the people in front of us, we would always remember that night at Wal-Mart, and remember that you never know what kind of day the people around you have had.

POINTS TO PONDER

- **Describe a time when God has sent a "Ms. Ruby" to encourage you.**

- **What does it mean for you to "cast all your cares" on Jesus? How does that change your thoughts and actions?**

- **Describe a time when the faith of others has carried you during moments of doubt?**

The Great Physician

"You made all the delicate, inner parts of my body and knit me together in my mother's womb. Thank you for making me so wonderfully complex! Your workmanship is marvelous- how well I know it. You watched me as I was being formed in utter seclusion, as I was woven together in the dark of the womb. You saw me before I was born. Every day of my life was recorded in your book. Every moment was laid out before a single day had passed."

Psalm 139:13-16(NLT)

Rick was awake and trying to follow activity in the room the next morning. His face was still very lop-sided, with little movement on the left side of his body. His breathing machine hummed away in the corner of the room, Rick's chest rising and falling with each pulsation of the machine. He was beginning to assist the ventilator, taking short breaths of his own in between the breaths that the machine delivered. It was hard to describe the look in Rick's eyes. There was a wild, disoriented appearance. It made looking at him a little frightening. There was no way to tell what he was thinking…did he understand what had happened to him…where he was? He looked frantically around the room. Phillip stroked the strands of hair back on his bruised forehead as I leaned in again to try to orient him to his surroundings. Both of his hands had been restrained to the bedrail in an effort to keep all of the lines and tubes in place. Pulling occasionally against the restraints, Rick looked helplessly at Phillip and me, slightly shrugging his shoulders as if to say, "What's the deal with all of this stuff??" Leaning in towards Rick, Phillip spoke to him quietly and calmly. I have always loved the sound of my husband's voice, and that moment was no exception. He was tender and calming as he tried to explain to Rick all that was going on. Rick listened with a blank stare on his face. Looking around the room for a minute or two, he seemed to relax again into the softness of the pillow that Phillip had fluffed under his head. His eyes slowly closed and Phillip and I were once again enveloped in the beeps and hums of all of the machines sustaining Rick's life.

Phillip went back out to the waiting room to visit with folks from Aiken that had begun to arrive. He was also on the phone back and forth with some of the church staff, continuing to try to manage and shepherd the church from the ICU waiting room. I was proud of him and so respectful of him at that moment, as both my husband and my pastor. He was continuing to be my steady oar.

As Phillip continued with his pastor-shepherd duties in the waiting room, I sat quietly at Rick's bedside for the rest of the morning and well into the afternoon hours. The nurses had grown accustomed to me and I was trying to get to know them a little bit, as well. Conversing with them about their own children, I hoped that it would give them a special connection to Rick and me, facilitating the quality of care that they gave to us. As an old ICU nurse, I knew that their job was very stressful, too. Maybe there would be some way that I could encourage and support them as they cared for Rick. Like wringing out a wet dish rag, I was becoming more and more determined to see God use every single bit of this horrible situation for His good.

Walking from one side of Rick's bed to the other, I did a visible check of every single machine, line or device that was entering or exiting his still swollen and bruised frame. His heart rate, blood pressure, oxygen saturation and heart rhythm were all normal…ventilator setting still all the same…subclavian line looked fine with IV Vancomycin running as ordered…both chest tubes were draining…still too much drainage though, I thought…foley catheter in place...sutures to Rick's forehead and left forearm were approximating well…wrist restraints not too tight…UGH, I thought, what am I doing?! I am not the nurse on duty!! I am the mom this time.

Rick slowly opened his eyes, almost as though he had heard me talking out loud. He somehow seemed more awake now. His eyes seemed a little clearer. I looked at him intently as he gazed back at me…like "no big deal…nothing much going on today" kind of way. I continued to watch him curiously, wondering what in the world he was thinking. He looked…well he looked pretty calm…he looked pretty much like Rick Lee! He slowly and methodically looked around the room…looked back at me and just kind of flipped his hand up, as if to ask, "What is all of this stuff?" I could see his hands moving a bit under the sheets so I pulled the covers back so that I could check all of his tubes again. As I pulled the sheet back, he raised his hand as much as the soft wrist restraint would allow and he motioned for something to drink. Not believing what I had seen, I leaned in and asked "Rick, do you need something?" He made the motion again for something to drink. Re-orienting Rick to the surroundings and why he was in the hospital, he continued to look at me and turned his head briefly to look at the machines that surrounded him. Slightly shrugging his shoulders, he laid there quietly for a minute, watching one of the nurses as she entered his room.

"Where's Chipper?" he mouthed slowly.

"Rick, your dog is fine. Chipper is at your house and he is being taken care of," I said, laughing out loud as I pulled the sheets back up around his shoulders.

As Rick drifted back off to sleep, I perched on the stool right beside his bed. We had been waiting all morning on the results of the MRI that had been done on Rick's brain the day before. I knew that the doctors were expecting for it to confirm the suspicion that Rick had suffered a diffuse axonal brain injury (DAI), an injury that results from the traumatic shearing forces that occur when the head is rapidly accelerated or decelerated. That type of injury usually does not have a good prognosis. Over ninety percent of patients with a DAI remain significantly impaired and never return to a normal level of functioning or have any semblance of independent living. They may remain vegetative or have very limited mobility, requiring total care for the rest of their lives. There are three levels of DAI: mild, moderate, or severe. We had already been told that Rick's head injury was severe. But I began to see a very different picture as I sat beside Rick's bed that day. I began to see very real, normal glimpses of my son. Rick began to tuck one leg under the other to sleep just like he did when he was a little boy….and he tried as hard as he could to raise his arm, attempting to place one hand behind his head while he slept. I knew what he was trying to do. A mother knows the way her children sleep. I grew more and more convinced that God was working in a huge way right before my very eyes.

I slumped back in the chair for a little while, allowing my mind to drift outside the walls of Palmetto Richland Hospital. As though I had pushed rewind on a video I was watching, I could see myself sitting in an old wooden rocking chair, singing to any one of the five of our children….“Before you had a name, or opened up your eyes, or anyone could recognize your face…you were being formed so delicate in size, secluded in God's safe and hidden place...with your little tiny hands and little tiny feet, and little eyes that shimmered like a pearl…He breathed in you a song…and to make the song complete, He brought the masterpiece into the world...You are a Masterpiece…a new creation he has formed…and you're as soft and fresh, as a snowy-winter morn…and I'm so glad that God has given you to me…little lamb from God…you are a masterpiece.”

Tears began to sprinkle the sheets on Rick's bed as I finished humming the song to myself. I sat there motionless and barely breathing for a minute; mesmerized by the words I was suddenly remembering…“you knit me together in my mother's womb”…those words came pouring into my thoughts, completely drowning out every alarm and hum of all the machines in the ICU. God's Word spoke louder and more audible that day than anything I have ever heard.

As a nurse, I believe that the brain and neurological system are the most delicate and intricate parts of the human body. That was evidenced by the fact that Rick's doctors were unable to predict the likelihood or extent of Rick's recovery. However, on that particular day, my nursing knowledge intersected with my faith. My nursing knowledge collided with the truth of scripture and gave me the hope and belief that I needed at that desperate moment. In the still and quiet of Rick's hospital room, I cried out to God with more desperation and earnestness than I have ever experienced in my entire life. I believed Psalm 139:13-16 with my whole heart that day. I had read those verses so many times over the years, but on that particular day, I claimed them to be real and true in a very personal way. I knew that God had created Rick in the secluded place of my womb. He had knit Rick together. I begged Him to knit him back together. I begged. I was desperate for God's presence and power….and I suddenly felt no more fear.

As I continued to have a simple sentence prayer conversation with God, claiming those verses, another Bible story that I have heard a hundred times came into my thoughts. I do not believe that it was coincidental. Jesus was visiting in a home in Capernaum. The home became packed with visitors and there was no more room inside or outside the house. Four men arrived at the home, carrying a paralyzed man on a mat. They couldn't bring him to Jesus because of the crowd, so they made a hole in the roof above His head. Then they lowered the man on his mat, right down in front of Jesus. And Jesus healed the man.

How many times have I read or heard that story? But on that day, God's Word became living and breathing to me. I closed my eyes and cut a hole in the roof. In my mind, I removed all the tubes, the wires, the gadgets, the beeps, the buzzes, the alarms, the doctors and nurses…and I removed myself…and I lowered my son through the roof and placed him at the feet of Jesus.

Soaring like Eagles

"But those who trust in the Lord will find new strength. They will soar high on wings like eagles. They will run and not grow weary. They will walk and not faint."
Isaiah 40:31

Phillip and I continued to sit all day at the hospital waiting on the doctors to report on the MRI results. Sharing with Phillip what I had observed of Rick during the afternoon, I told him that I believed with all my heart that Rick was improving. Rick seemed more and more alert and aware of things every time he woke up. He was also beginning to indicate pain when he tried to move his shoulder, grimacing with the slightest movement of this left side.

Several nurses came in and told us that they wanted to try to get Rick up into a chair. Explaining that they would prop his head if he were not able to support it, they continued to explain that it would also help his lungs if he sat in the recliner for a little while. With two nurses, a physical therapist, and a mother watching like a hawk from the corner of the room, they slowly prepared Rick for the transfer from bed to recliner. Every tube, line and device had to be repositioned multiple times. With every move Rick's face looked as though someone was stabbing him. With continued limited facial movement on the left side, it was still a little frightening to look at Rick. Inch by inch, after about thirty minutes of maneuvering, Rick was finally "sitting" in the large special recliner that the physical therapist had brought into his room. For brief intervals, Rick would lift his head and support its weight as he attempted to look around the room. He looked completely exhausted after the slightest attempts of any movement. Sitting in the chair seemed to trigger more coughing episodes, which continuously seemed to set off the alarms on the ventilator. I wondered if Rick realized or understood that he was connected to a breathing machine. When the alarms sounded, he would look at the machine, look at me, and just shrug his shoulders. I saw that as very "Rick-ish" though. Rick had always had a very even temperament ….was always pretty calm and laid back. Nothing really ever upset Rick too much. I continued to believe that I was seeing real glimpses of the real Rick. I was totally convinced of that.

The doctors finally came in late that afternoon with the MRI report. Holding the hard copy in their hand, they nodded at Rick and began talking to Phillip and me about the results.

"The MRI confirms what we were expecting. Rick has multiple areas of hemorrhage in the brain, a fractured temporal bone and has sustained a diffuse axonal brain injury," the doctor said, pausing for a moment. As the doctor paused, Rick looked at all of us and slightly shrugged his shoulders, as if to say, "What did he say?" Then he motioned for something to drink! Phillip and I laughed and the doctor looked at us as though we were being inappropriate. I explained that Rick had been doing that all afternoon, as well as beginning to follow more and more simple commands when asked. The doctor shook his head, almost in disbelief, looking at the hard copy report that he was holding in his hand. "What we are seeing just doesn't match up," continued the doctor. "Rick has sustained a very serious, severe head injury. Clinically though, he is already well beyond the point that we would expect him to recover."

Phillip and I nodded our heads, smiling at each other and gripping hands. "He is being knit back together," I said softly, squeezing Phillip's hand as tears rolled down my face. Rick just sat there looking at all of us, one eye open and one eye half-closed!

The case manager and one of Rick's nurses came in shortly after that, discussing the possibility of transferring him to Shepherd Center in Atlanta.

"Shepherd Center is one of the top rehabilitation hospitals in the country, specializing in brain and spinal cord injuries. We believe that's where Rick needs to go next, but it may be difficult to get a bed at that facility. The Assessment Coordinator from Shepherd will be here tomorrow to see another patient. Is it all right if we try to get her to do an assessment of Rick's condition at the same time?" the case manager asked.

"Absolutely" Phillip said.

They quickly left the room to set all of the details in motion. We turned back to Rick, and he made a gesture with his hand, trying to ask what was going on. Sitting on the edge of his bed and leaning in close, we tried to explain what the plans were. He looked nonchalantly back and forth at us, shrugged, and then motioned for something to drink again. The more awake and alert Rick became, the more difficult it was to explain and ascertain how much he understood. Telling him that he had a tube going to his stomach seemed to frustrate him. Rolling his eyes a little with my response, he let his head fall back on the pillow. We knew that it was impossible and unreasonable to expect him to understand what we were telling him. We decided it was better to opt for short answers with little detail for the time being. I was thankful when the staff finally came to put him back in the bed. It was an exhausting and painful process just to watch. With Rick finally settled back in bed and sleeping quietly, Phillip and I left the hospital to rest and prepare for our encounter planned for the next day.

Early the next morning, we arrived back at Palmetto Richland, eager to meet the representative from Shepherd Center. She arrived at eleven o'clock, right on schedule. Phillip and I were both feeling a little anxious, not knowing what kinds of questions to expect or what would be involved in getting Rick placed in Atlanta. Her assessment of Rick was extremely thorough, discussing every detail of his medical care with the nurses and doctors involved in Rick's case. She then turned her attention to Phillip and me, asking questions about our home and family.

"I need to know about the physical layout of your home and about the people that will be there to help take care of

Rick," she said. "We don't know what the extent of his recovery will be, even if we are able to get him placed at Shepherd Center. We have to be sure that Rick will have a place to go and resources for his care at the time of discharge from Shepherd before we can even accept him as a patient to begin rehabilitation." She spoke quietly, but with care, as she looked at both of us, waiting patiently for one of us to respond.

"We will do whatever we need to," I said without hesitation. "We have a large, very close family and we will do what we need to. Please just help us get him there to begin rehab." I looked right into her eyes as I made my plea and her gaze lingered on mine for a minute. I wondered what she was thinking as she "evaluated" us. Her job must be very difficult, especially when she ends up telling families that a patient does not meet criteria for admission. She asked a few more questions and then told us that she needed to go look at Rick's chart. As she left the room, Phillip and I exchanged nervous glances. What would be our options if Shepherd Center would not take Rick? We did not have to ponder that question for long. The case manager and the representative from Shepherd Center came back into Rick's room about thirty minutes later with the answers we were waiting for.

"We have a bed at Shepherd Center for Rick and we would like to try to arrange the transfer for tomorrow morning. It will be an air ambulance flight from Columbia to Atlanta, ICU to ICU transfer. We will allow two family members to fly with Rick during the transport. We will need other family members to bring a list of personal items that he will need once he is at Shepherd Center. I know that this is a lot of information and that this is all happening very fast for you. The sooner we can get Rick to Atlanta, the better," the case manager concluded.

Phillip and I nodded at each other and at the case manager, both reaching for our cell phones to update the children and folks at church about the details. It was as though someone had pushed the fast-forward button on a DVD player.

Phillip and I were also contemplating so many financial decisions at any given moment. The air ambulance transport company required a large sum up front to fly Rick from Columbia to Atlanta. I looked worriedly at Phillip as we got that news because I knew that we did not have the money. Once again, we were overwhelmed with gratitude for the CCC family. The church's senior leadership team had decided to sell orange armbands that said "Thumbs Up, Pray for Rick" in an effort to help us with the financial expenses that were mounting. Phillip reminded me that the arm band money could possibly be used to transport Rick.

"You let me deal with those details and you take care of Rick," Phillip said gently, but emphatically. I took him up on that offer.

We had also been having discussions about what to do regarding Rick's finances. Rick had graduated from Clemson in May, and at that time assumed car insurance and cell phone payments by automatic draft from his account. Not wanting his accounts or bills to be delinquent, Phillip had talked to John Travis, the financial counselor from the church. That afternoon, we witnessed one of the most amazing things seen since the accident had occurred. John Travis, lawyer Ray Massey, and a notary came into Rick's room to obtain Power of Attorney so that we could access all of Rick's financial information and make sure his bills were paid. Ray told Phillip to explain what we were trying to do and that if Rick could indicate that he understood by following simple commands, then the Power of Attorney would be granted. As Ray, John and the notary walked into Rick's room, it was as though Rick recognized or knew that men of distinction had just walked into his room. Attempting to lean forward, Rick extended his hand to shake their hands! I was amazed. I looked at John and said, "It's a miracle John! I think we are seeing a miracle!" John and I both stood there for a few minutes watching Rick, tears in our eyes. John Travis is a wonderful person.

As Phillip explained to Rick what we were trying to do, he asked Rick if he understood what he was saying. Rick gave a quick "thumbs up" and then mouthed "thank you" to John and to Ray. It was a priceless moment for everyone in the room. We were so, so thankful for those gentlemen that afternoon and especially for John, as he helped advise us in so many ways regarding all of Rick's personal finances and medical bills.

What a day it had been! We were soaring like eagles that night as we left the hospital. Our strength and hope had been renewed by loving friends, so many answers to prayer, and by such positive signs from Rick. We knew that God would once again renew our strength as we prepared ourselves for transport to Atlanta the next day.

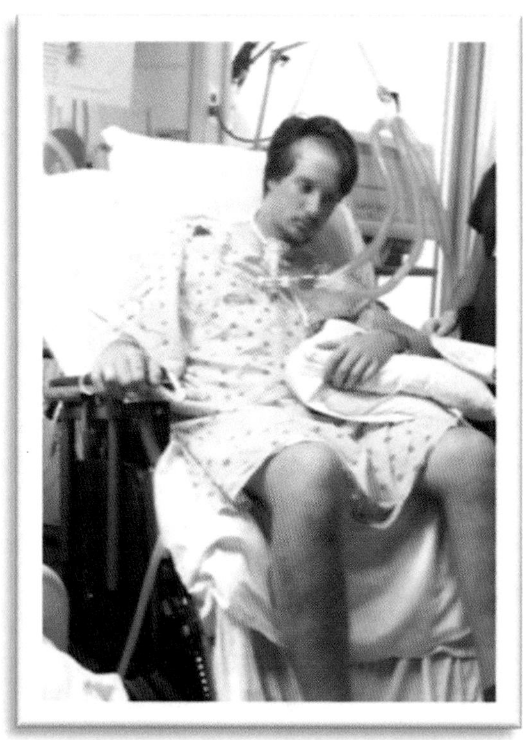

Sitting up for the first time!

Mission Trip

"The Lord is my light and my salvation, so why should I be afraid? The Lord is my fortress, protecting me from danger, so why should I tremble?"
Psalm 27:1

I despise flying! I have been to Africa and India on mission trips and the travel time has always been my least favorite part of the experience. It absolutely mortifies me to look out of the window on the plane. Flying home from Uganda, the pilot came over the loud speaker announcing that we were flying over the Sahara Desert, informing us that he was lowering our altitude just a bit so that we could get a good view from our seats. I was not the least bit excited!!

Waking up very early the next morning, I laid there for a little while listening to the sound of Phillip's peaceful, steady breathing as he slept next to me. Phillip and I had decided that Emily and I would fly in transport with Rick to Shepherd Center. He was planning to go by Rick's house on the way to Atlanta to pick up several things that the case manager told us Rick would need once he arrived. I laid there wondering how Emily would do with the flight to Atlanta. She had never flown before but was absolutely determined to accompany Rick and me that day. She is tough and typically very stoic. Phillip and I decided not to argue with her. We could tell this was something she needed to do.

Startled by the sudden sound of the alarm clock, we sprang into action. We had slept at Phillip's brother's house that night, about twenty minutes from the hospital. The flight team was scheduled to arrive at Palmetto Richland at eight o'clock, but Phillip and I had planned to get there with Emily around six-thirty so that we were there as they prepared Rick for transport.

As I showered, I was immediately aware of a queasy feeling growing in the pit of my stomach. My fear of flying came cascading into my thoughts like beads of water falling from the shower head. God help me do this today, I thought, as I rinsed the soap from my hair. I knew this would be the most important mission trip I had ever been on.

"Em, you ok?" I asked, as Emily threw her bag into the car.

"Yep, let's go," she said, never hesitating with her answer. Backing out of the driveway, Phillip and I began going over the list of things that he would pick up at Wal-Mart and at Rick's house. We had still not been back to Aiken since the night of the accident, so I quickly ran over a list of things for him to grab from home. We rode in silence the rest of the way to the hospital. I wondered how long it would be before we would be going home again. Our life has changed forever, I thought, straining to hold back the tears that suddenly flooded my eyes. Think about the task at hand, Terry. Stay focused.

Arriving at the hospital, we went straight up to ICU. Rick was awake and there was quite a buzz of activity around his bed. Still unable to communicate because of the breathing tube, he shrugged his shoulders, as if to ask, "What's going on?" Starting from the very beginning, for probably the one-hundredth time, Phillip leaned in to gently remind Rick that he had wrecked his truck and was in the hospital.

"You are being transferred to Atlanta today, Rick. You are going to fly on an airplane. Emily and I are going with you," I said calmly. Thank you, Lord, I whispered to myself. I knew that God was giving me strength and confidence, even though my stomach continued to tell me otherwise.

Like a cavalry arriving for a gun fight, the flight team appeared from around the corner. As though the Red Sea had just been parted, they were given immediate and swift access to Rick. Phillip, Emily, and I quickly got out of the way, but were allowed to remain in the hallway, watching as the team prepared Rick for travel. The flight team worked like a well-oiled machine. Barely speaking to one another, their actions were very intentional and precise. There was a huge amount of equipment to manage, as well as all of the lines, tubes, drains, and devices that were still being used to care for Rick. None of it could be left behind. I suddenly became aware of my heart pounding in my chest. Forcing myself to take a few slow deep breaths, I grabbed Phillip's hand, instantly feeling the stabilizing force that he had provided me during many years of marriage. Rick grimaced and shook his head as they tugged and pulled on him, trying to get him into the right position to transfer him onto the flight stretcher. Once transferred, they strapped Rick to the stretcher, checking every piece of equipment one more time, making sure every line and tube was secure.

"Who's going with us?" the critical care flight nurse asked suddenly.

"Emily and I are," I replied quickly. "I am his mom and I am a nurse," I said.

"Not on this flight," she said authoritatively. "And only one of you can go," she said, as she handed me a stack of papers to sign.

My heart broke as I saw the disappointed look on Emily's face, but there was no time to coddle her. Hugging Phillip and Emily tightly, I fell in behind the entourage of staff assisting with Rick's transport. Down the back elevator and out to a loading ramp, I stood and watched as they hoisted Rick's stretcher up into the ambulance. Not knowing exactly what to do, I walked around to the side of the ambulance to stand out of the way until I was given further instructions. Glancing up at the side of the ambulance I was completely surprised at what I saw. There was a huge gold cross painted on the side of the ambulance, with the words "Gold Cross Ambulance Service" painted around the cross. I smiled and shook my head. Flipping my cell phone out, I quickly took a picture of the cross and sent it to Phillip and Emily with a text…."We are fine….God is with us….I am not afraid." And with that, my stomach finally settled down.

Having been instructed to climb up into the right passenger's seat, I sat waiting for the flight team to finish securing Rick into place for transport to the air strip. There was a large rear-view mirror that allowed people riding in the front of the ambulance to see all of the activity in the patient care area. That was a huge blessing to me as we headed down the road towards the airport.

"He's doing fine, Mom," the flight nurse called from the back of the ambulance. "Everything looks good."

Arriving at the air strip, fast-forward activity occurred again, with the team intent and very task-oriented. Methodically, but swiftly making the transfer from ambulance to aircraft, the flight team prepared for take-off. Looking around the small prop plane, I understood why the flight nurse said that only one family member could come. The nurse and the paramedic sat facing Rick's stretcher, continuously monitoring every part of Rick's care. I sat just behind Rick's head, with my back to the cock-pit. Looking over my right shoulder, my eyes briefly met those of the pilot. He had soft, caring eyes and a very grandfather-type demeanor. I felt very cared for just by his glance.

"Thank you for taking us," I said quietly. He nodded and said that we would be in Atlanta in about forty-five minutes. With that, I turned my attention back to Rick. He was trying to look around the plane, almost as though he was trying to figure out where he was. There was kind of a wild, confused look in his eyes and I knew that in the very least he was probably disoriented with the transfer. Leaning forward, I was able to place my hands on his head and talk to him quietly as the plane rolled down the runway. Once in the air, I unbuckled my seatbelt and was able to lean forward where Rick could see my face. Re-orienting him again, his respiration and heart rate slowed down a little bit and he seemed a little more relaxed.

"You're ok Rick," I said gently. "We're both ok."

I realized that I was looking out the window, watching the soft, white clouds envelop the plane. For just a moment, I allowed myself to feel the peace that the fluffy clouds and the constant hum of the plane engine offered. I knew that Rick and I were safe and protected.

Approximately thirty minutes into the flight, Rick became anxious and agitated. He was trying to wrench his hands loose and would look over his head at me trying to talk. His respiratory rate and heart rate increased again and the flight nurse decided it was time to give him medication for pain and anxiety. Explaining that we could not risk losing any of his lines or tubes while in flight, he had to remain tightly restrained on the stretcher. I was so thankful when the medication took effect and Rick eased off to sleep. We talked about our nursing experience during the remainder of the flight and before I knew it, the pilot was instructing me to buckle back up for landing. The flight had been much shorter, needless to say, than my other mission trips, but this mission trip was far from over. I knew that very well.

From the airstrip, to once again on board an ambulance, we sped towards Shepherd Center, dodging in between the cars engulfed in the Atlanta traffic. Texting Phillip to let him know we were on the ground again, I received a text back from him saying he and Emily had picked up all that Rick and I needed from home and were headed towards Atlanta. Making small talk with the ambulance driver, I was relieved when we finally pulled up in front of a large building with "Shepherd Center" written boldly on the side. This will be home for a while, I thought, as they lowered Rick's stretcher to the ground. His eyes were closed now, still snoozing from the sedation that he had received during the flight. I stood just behind the ambulance, watching eagerly as the flight crew prepared Rick for entrance into his home away from home. As the stretcher moved forward, I fell in behind again, but was totally unprepared for what I was about to see on the inside of this new place that my son and I were entering.

Pausing for barely a few seconds at the front desk, the flight crew rolled right on down the hallway. The stretcher rolled easily on the shiny tiled floor, the chest tube drainage compartments clanging occasionally against the sides of the bed. It was a long hallway and pictures hanging on either side of the wall began to catch my eye and overwhelm me. There were so many pictures.... so many faces....former patients and their families....people in wheelchairs....people with trachs and helmets on...people with all kinds of gadgets and contraptions for breathing and for walking....people in harnesses and braces....people lying down or barely sitting up...... I realized all of a sudden that I was totally unprepared to enter that place....to see all of that. It frightened me. I wanted to scream. I wanted to run. Oh God, what is this place??!! Oh God, help me. I can't do this!

Finally at the elevator, I leaned for a moment against the wall, silently wishing that as I leaned against it a magic door would open and allow me to escape from the nightmare. The only door that opened was that of the elevator, waiting to take us up to the Intensive Care Unit on the fourth floor.

"We'll have to wait on the next one," the flight nurse said as the elevator quickly filled with wheelchairs and other family members.

It seemed to take forever, and it seemed that everyone walking by was staring at my son. One man sat quietly in his wheelchair, powered only by his own breath blowing into a small tube that was connected from somewhere behind his chair. His hands and fingers were in a crumpled mess, lying motionless in his lap. I tried desperately to smile at him, but was forced to look away without even making eye contact, so afraid that he would see the horror and fear that I was feeling. God, this is the worst place I have ever been, I thought. God, how am I going to do this?

Finally arriving on the fourth floor, Rick was whisked away behind the double doors of the Intensive Care Unit and I was instructed to sit in a small room to wait for the Admission Representative. I forced myself to think mean, angry thoughts, hoping that would help me bridle back the flood of tears that I tried desperately to control. Hold it together, Terry. Phillip is on the way. And with that, the first of many people came into the room with endless stacks of papers and instructions.

"I am from the Disability Office," the first man announced.

Disability? What the hell are you talking about, I thought? Nobody needs disability!!!!! Now I did not need to pretend that I was having mean and angry thoughts!

"We are required to fill out this paperwork for every patient," he continued. "Rick will be re-evaluated after ninety days to see if he qualifies. For now, we just need to get him into the system."

I signed, and signed, and then signed some more. I read nothing. I was totally numb and scared to death. As one person after another came in with their papers and instructions, I was completely saturated with information and in total sensory overload. I tried to comprehend what they were saying but it felt like I was listening to someone talk under water.....like static on a radio. Once the last paper was signed and that person had disappeared around the corner, I walked into the restroom nearby and finally let my stomach have its way.

POINTS TO PONDER

- **What passage(s) of Scripture have been most significant to you in your life?**

- **In what ways do you believe that you are "fearfully and wonderfully made?"**

- **Describe a time when you felt desperate? Who or what did you cry out to in that desperate moment?**

- **Isaiah 40:31 compares trusting in God to an eagle flying. What aspects of that word picture helps you better understand trust?**

- **What is one of your greatest fears and has there ever been a time when you have been forced to face it?**

Shock and Awe

"I am worn out from sobbing. All night I flooded my bed with weeping, drenched it with tears. My vision is blurred by grief."
Psalm 6:6

Phillip and Emily arrived just as I was going back to see Rick in the Intensive Care Unit. Quickly debriefing on what had occurred over the past several hours, we hurried on into Rick's room to see if there had been any changes in his condition since arriving at Shepherd Center. He seemed to be resting quietly, opening his eyes at intervals to gaze around the room. Rick still had chest tubes on the right and left sides, but his respiratory status was really beginning to improve. He was requiring much less assistance from the breathing machine and we were very encouraged to hear that they were beginning to consider weaning him completely off of the machine. We were very hopeful of that.

The end of the day finally came and Rick was sleeping quietly in his new bed at Shepherd Center. We decided to end our day as well, heading over to the small apartment complex attached to the hospital that was provided for family members. Our living space was comprised of a small kitchen-den combo with a table for four and a small two-person couch. The adjoining room had two twin beds and the bathroom was nestled in between those two areas. Walking into the bathroom, I was once again faced with the stark reality of our circumstances. The entire bathroom was handicap accessible, with high toilet seat, low sink, and pull bars all over the walls. I closed my eyes and shuddered a little bit as I thought about the man in the wheelchair. I pulled out a stack of papers that the disability man had left for us to look at.....how wide are the doors going into your home?......how many steps are there at each entrance/exit?.....tubs or showers?.....upstairs/down stairs?...... It asked for measurements and details regarding every area of our home. Collapsing onto the little couch and throwing the papers in the middle of the floor, the dam finally broke and the flood of tears was released. We cried until the well went dry, and then just sat in silence. Every imaginable emotion had been felt on that day. We were poured out and empty. There was nowhere else to go but to bed.

We got up early the next morning and went back over to Rick's room. Phillip Jr. and Katelyn were coming from Aiken and Rebecca was bringing Ben from Anderson. I was anxious to have everyone together again, even if it was just to huddle around Rick's bed.

We spent all day in and out of Rick's room, encouraged by the number of waking hours that he had and also by the extent that he tried to follow activity around his room. His facial expression was still very lop-sided but he followed simple commands very well and gave us a "thumbs up" often. The occupational and physical therapist came in to assess Rick and measured him for a special wheelchair that would be used to get him out of bed during the day. It took an hour to get Rick up and positioned with all of his tubes. Chest tubes with drainage containers hung from each side of the wheelchair, the catheter that drained his bladder was also put strategically in just the right place. The feeding tube that went to his stomach was taped in place so that it would not get inadvertently tugged on, and special care had to also be exercised in handling Rick's PICC line (peripherally inserted central catheter) for his intravenous medication administration. Once all those tubes and lines had been negotiated, meticulous attention was also paid to the trach area and his oxygen saturation, making sure that his respiratory status had not been compromised during the transfer from bed to chair.

Once Rick was safely in the wheelchair, the therapist taught me how to do a "weight shift" with Rick. Once an hour, warning Rick ahead of time that we were getting ready to move his chair, the entire wheelchair would be tilted backwards for sixty seconds, allowing Rick's weight to shift off of the bony prominences in the hips and buttocks area. This protected Rick from getting skin breakdown in those areas because of his limited mobility and decreased circulation. Despite our forewarning, the procedure always startled Rick and caused a huge grimace on his face. I knew it had to be done but that did not make it any easier to do the maneuver.

Rick seemed to hate sitting up in the wheelchair. His arms and legs flopped around and he still did not have the strength to hold his head up for any length of time. Everyday got a little bit better though. It was still hard for us to discern how much he understood. He would follow simple commands but then look wildly around the room as though he did not know where he was. Each of us continued to spend time during each visit re-orienting Rick to the surroundings, only to have him wake from a nap disoriented again. It was a maddening, exhausting cycle for all of us.

We retreated back to the little apartment to rest for another night. We slept all together, with foam mattresses and pillows thrown all over the floor. Family pictures from home had been sprinkled around the room and snack food and soda cans covered the little kitchen countertop. It felt very much like a college dorm room. It felt safe and secure. I knew that all my chickens were in the coop and I felt a small measure of peace as I fell off to sleep that night.

Right back in Rick's room early the next morning, we were all thrilled to hear that he had a great night on minimal ventilator support, so they had decided to remove him from the breathing machine to see how he would do during the day. The speech therapist also came by to let us know that they were going to put a red button or "voice valve" on Rick's trach allowing him to speak in an audible voice rather than attempting to simply mouth all of his words. We were so excited. The voice valve went on and we all waited expectantly to hear Rick speak. With eyes open wide and all leaning slightly forward straining to hear, we must have looked like a bunch of kids waiting to see Santa! Finally, after a couple of forceful coughs, Rick mumbled, "Where's Chipper?" I think we all laughed and cried at the same time!

There was a steady stream of therapists coming in all morning long. Even though Rick was still in ICU, they allowed all of us to stay in his room. Hearing his voice had been like a shot of adrenalin for all of us. We all took turns trying to talk to Rick. He answered some of our questions that were simple with a very flat affect, no emotion or inflection in his voice at all. At times he would just stare off in the distance as though he had not heard us. Then something happened that scared all of us and it set the tone for the rest of the day.

Before Rick had the voice valve, he would occasionally motion for something to drink. Now he was able to ask audibly for something to drink.

"I want a Mountain Dew," Rick said evenly, again with no emotion whatsoever.

"Rick, you aren't able to eat or drink anything yet," I explained. We all laughed a little at his request and then started chattering amongst ourselves again. All of a sudden, Rick leaned forward in his bed and started banging on the bedrails.

"Guys, I said get me a Mountain Dew," he screamed. Total silence fell over the room as we all looked at Rick, realizing that he was very serious. Becoming more agitated, Rick looked wildly around the room at each of us, shaking his head back and forth.

"Rick, do you remember where you are?" I asked, easing a little closer to his bed, trying to talk in a soft, soothing voice.

"Yea," he said. "I'm in England." His head fell back on the pillow and he stared blankly past all of us.

There remained a total hush in the room that afternoon as Rick thrashed in the bed and talked wildly out of his head. We took turns staying with him, trying to keep him oriented. It was a horribly frightening experience. The doctors and nurses told us to keep conversation very simple and quiet, hopefully decreasing the agitation that Rick was exhibiting. Finally, after restraining Rick's hands to the bed and giving him medication through his PICC line, he eased off to sleep.

"Does he have to stay restrained if I am in the room with him?" I asked the nurse.

"If you are in the room, he can be unrestrained. But it is bedtime and you cannot stay in the ICU at night. He will have to stay restrained for now," she said.

I stood in the doorway watching Rick sleep. Tears streamed down my face as I shrugged helplessly at Phillip. A day that had started with feelings of elation was ending with feelings of frustration and despair. We meandered our way in silence through the hallways of the hospital, ending up on the roof that overlooked the Atlanta skyline.

"Is he gonna be like this forever, Mom?" asked Phillip Jr., tears coming down his face now, as well.

"I don't know buddy," I replied quietly. "There is no way of knowing. We will just take one day at a time. That's all we can do."

We sat on the roof in silence for quite a while that night, watching the Atlanta traffic crawl like ants far below. I found myself wondering how many other families had been on that same roof at one time or another, crying out into the cool night air for answers to questions that no one but God could know.

Phillip and Emily at Shepherd Center

Determined to Succeed

"Commit your actions to the Lord, and your plans will succeed. The Lord has made everything for his own purposes."
Proverbs 16:3-4

It was Sunday and Phillip and I had decisions to make. He had been away from home for almost two weeks now. Katelyn had been out of school and he had been away from the church. The entire church staff was doing a fantastic job, but we knew that he could not be gone indefinitely and that Katelyn needed to go back to Aiken, as well. The other definite thing that both of us knew was that I was not leaving Rick. I knew what to watch for….the things to monitor when the nurses were not in the room….and I was not leaving. So we made the decision together and stuck to it. That afternoon, Rebecca headed back to Anderson with Ben. Phillip and the rest of the kids loaded up and headed for Aiken. Phillip was determined and focused on taking care of Katelyn, keeping his hand on the pulse of the other kids, and getting back to shepherd the folks at Cedar Creek Church. And I was just as determined and focused to use the gifts and talents that God had given me to help care for Rick. My mother's motto, underneath her picture in her college nursing annual reads: "The surest way not to fail is to determine to succeed." We were all determined.

Watching the car pull out of the parking garage, I felt sad, but resolved, as I walked back into the hospital. We had no idea what the coming days and weeks would hold, but we all knew that we had a function and a purpose that was vital as the story continued to unfold. I was so proud of the leadership that Phillip gave our entire family and I was immeasurably proud of the strength and courage that our children continued to demonstrate on a daily basis.

Getting back up to Rick's room, he glanced at me briefly as I entered, fumbling with the sheet beneath his fingers. "Get these things off," he said flatly, nodding at the wrist restraints.

"Rick, do you know where you are," I asked quietly, slowly untying one of the restraints.

"Yea, I'm in Germany," he replied, with neither his facial expression nor tone of voice changing in the least.

"Rick, you are in the hospital in Atlanta. You wrecked your truck. I'm here with you and I'm not leaving," I said, looking directly into his eyes.

He remained silent as I untied the other restraint. Placing both of his hands on top of the sheets where I could see them, I pulled a chair over so that I could sit right next to the bed. The ICU beds at Shepherd Center had TV monitors attached to the headboard that allowed the TVs to be pulled forward and placed right in front of the patient's face. That seemed to be a huge blessing for Rick. He watched Sunday afternoon football all day long.

"Mom, call Dad," Rick said.

"Why Rick?" I replied.

"He's got to order my football gear. I've got a game next week," Rick said, very matter-of-factly.

I nodded my head and smiled at him. He continued to stare at the TV. Sliding his hands quickly under the covers, he went right for the tubes.

"Rick, hands on top of the covers or I'll have to tie them down," I said firmly.

He shot me the bird and kept watching TV. I think at that particular moment he knew exactly what he was doing!

The speech therapist had come in earlier and had done a "swallow test" on Rick. He had passed with flying colors so she had given permission for him to have ice chips.

"Rick, do you want some ice chips," I asked, offering him a spoonful.

"Maybe in a minute," he said, continuing to stare at the TV.

I sat in silence for a little while, battling his hand movements every five or ten minutes. I was determined not to restrain him as long as I was sitting right beside him.

"Rick, don't touch the tubes," I said emphatically.

"Devil woman," he said. I shot him the bird! And so that is how the first day of my private-duty, most precious nursing assignment ever ended. Rick fell asleep watching football. I gently slipped the soft wrist restraints back into place and quietly left his room for the night.

Taking the elevator down to the first floor, I walked slowly down the corridor towards the apartment complex attached to Shepherd Center. Thinking about the deserted and somewhat barren room that I was returning to for the night, I slowed my steps and paused to look at the wall-to-wall pictures of previous patients that I was passing. Reading the captions beneath each picture, I began to realize the wide array of stories….the tragic circumstances that had led each of these folks to Shepherd Center. But as I stepped back from the wall, just scanning from one face to the next, there was one common feature that stood out above all others. They were all smiling. This is the most hopeful, yet depressing place I have ever been, I thought, as I continued on down the hallway.

Finally entering our apartment building for the night, I was immediately greeted by the deafening silence of the empty room. Flipping the light on, I was quickly reminded of the sheer number of bodies that we had crammed into the room to sleep. Thin, portable mattresses and covers lay all over the floor. Empty soda cans and Twinkie wrappers also lined the room from one end to the next. Breakfast of champions, I thought, as I began to clean our well littered living space. Walking over to the kitchen counter, I caught a glimpse of the stack of papers that I had tossed there late the night before. Disability papers…..pages and pages of information and questions. I read for a little while and filled in some of the blanks but then my mind shut down. I could feel myself getting angry. How do they know Rick is going to need any of this stuff…..Tom can build a wheelchair ramp….the bathrooms are not wide enough….how will I teach Phillip and the kids to suction and do tube feedings…..???.....Suddenly the stack of papers joined the soda cans and Twinkie wrappers already laying around the room. I will not fill those papers out, I thought definitively. I WILL NOT DO IT!

Slumping onto the small pull-out sofa, I laid there for a while, staring at the family photo that had been placed in the center of the kitchen table. I wondered if our family would ever look like that again. Would things ever be “normal” again? I closed my eyes and allowed my mind to rewind back to the days of playing volleyball in the front yard, floating on a raft at Clarks Hill Lake, and the endless times I have screamed and fussed at the kids to clean up their room. Opening my eyes again, I smiled a little as I looked around at the disarray. I’m gonna leave it like this, I thought. It makes me feel right at home.

Moving Day

"I rise early, before the sun is up; I cry out for help and put my hope in your words."
Psalm 119:147

I was back in Rick's room very early the next morning. The night nurse was still on duty so I approached her to ask what kind of night Rick had.

"He rested well," she replied. "The tube feeding is beginning to upset his stomach though. He is having diarrhea and so we have placed him in an adult diaper. Let us know if you need anything." Standing beside his bed, I reached down and gently began to loosen the soft wrist restraints that were in place. Opening his eyes briefly, he acknowledged that I was there with the nod of his head, quickly closing them again to drift back off to sleep. Rick would never, ever be an early riser unless he was forced to be. He loved to sleep! Pulling a chair up next to his bed, I was content with sitting quietly, watching the peaceful rise and fall of his chest as he breathed. I slowly began to survey all of his tubes, lines, and drains….the monitors….his tube feeding and his chest tubes. It is hard, if not impossible, to turn off the nursing part of my brain. As though I were assessing a patient at the beginning of one of my shifts, I inspected every aspect of Rick's care. Satisfied that everything looked within normal limits, I settled back down in the chair next to his bed.

The pulmonologist came in early to make rounds and I was very excited about the news that he shared. "Rick's right lung has continued to improve so I would like to discontinue the chest tube on the right side. We will keep the chest tube on the left side for another day or two, but if he does well, we will possibly move him out of ICU this afternoon."

The chest tube was removed, the morning flew by, and before I knew it, we were preparing to move Rick to another room.

"What room is he going to?" I asked the nurse, as she came in to hang his antibiotic.

"He is going to the ABI floor," she replied. She must have been able to read the question-mark look on my face.

"He is going to the Acquired Brain Injury Unit," the nurse continued. They specialize in the rehabilitation of patients with acquired brain injuries (ABI)….brain injuries that are acquired as the result of trauma or illness, not from birth," she concluded, just as she finished flushing Rick's IV line. "All the patients on that particular floor have brain injuries," she said, rather nonchalantly, I thought.

I could feel myself taking a slow deep breath, trying to steady my nerves. The sound of the words "brain injury" still made me want to run screaming through a plate-glass window, and the thought of Rick being on a floor with a brain injury, completely surrounded by others with the same condition, was overwhelming to me. I grabbed for my phone, calling Phillip quickly to update him on Rick's room change. I felt immediately steadied by his voice and was thankful to hear that he, Katelyn and the other kids were doing well.

"I will call you again tonight," I said quickly, as the nurses began to roll Rick's bed down the hallway. Down the elevator to the second floor, we rolled through double doors that had "ACQUIRED BRAIN INJURY" in huge letters above the door. Once on the unit, I was thrown into complete sensory overload. There were patients in wheel chairs all up and down the corridor, some just sitting and staring off into the distance, some pushing themselves around using their feet. There were several patients wearing helmets, exhibiting some type of seizure-like activity. Others had no helmets on, but it was evident that a portion of their skull had been removed, leaving the appearance of a head deformity in its place. Feeling nauseated, I put my head down and focused on the wheels turning on the bottom of Rick's stretcher. Arriving in his room, it took quite a while for the nurses to get Rick situated again. The move had evidently loosened a lot of secretions in Rick's chest, requiring several intervals of tracheal suctioning to get his oxygen saturation back to normal limits. The chest tube drainage system on the left, as well as the IV pumps and tube feeding pump had to be repositioned in the room. Rick looked confused and disoriented as they tried to settle him into his new bed and he made a horrible grimace every time he was moved from side to side.

"Hang in there, Rick," I said from the doorway, just trying to stay out of the way. Once the ordeal was over, I stood quietly beside Rick's bed, trying to orient him to the this new area.

"Rick, do you know where you are," I asked softly.

"Germany," he said. "And all these people are freakin' Nazis," he yelled.

"Rick you are in the hospital in Atlanta. You wrecked your truck. I am gonna stay with you."

He looked at me very matter-of-factly, picking at the bed covers, but unable to grasp them between his fingers. I repositioned the covers around his frail and now-deformed collar bone, trying to comfort him in any way that I could. I felt helpless. Sitting again in the chair beside his bed, I suddenly became aware of activity on the other side of the room. The curtain had been drawn so we had not been able to see the patient lying in the bed next to Rick. Now there was a commotion that was unavoidable. I could discern the banging and clanging noise of a wheelchair and also grunts and deep breathing coming from the other patient. I glanced nervously at Rick, wondering if any of the noises were disturbing or frightening to him. Rick just stared at the wall as though he had not heard anything at all. Suddenly, the curtain was pulled back and the other patient scooted by us in his wheelchair, nudging himself forward with the use of his feet. Pushing the door completely closed, the patient turned his wheelchair around to face Rick and I, grunting and staring at both of us. Caught completely off guard and still in sensory overload regarding the ABI unit, I was frightened and I felt defensive for Rick. I did not want that man sitting there staring at Rick and me. Why won't he go back onto his side of the room, I thought? What's he staring at?? I finally could not take it any longer. I got up and stood between Rick and the other patient, breaking the patient's line-of-sight. Becoming disinterested, the patient slowly pushed toward the door, opened the door, and exited the room, grunts audible all the way down the hallway. Rick appeared un-phased by the encounter and had closed his eyes and drifted back off to sleep. Making sure his hands were well restrained again, I left his bedside to find a place of retreat for a few minutes. My mind was completely saturated and I felt overwhelmed again.

Standing outside in the breezeway, my hand quickly dialed Phillip's cell phone. As soon as I heard his voice, I broke into sobbing, trying to explain the details of the afternoon and the inundation of sights and sounds that I had experienced during Rick's room transfer. I realized that we had been somewhat secluded and protected in the ICU environment, but my introduction to the ABI Unit had been shocking and abrasive….frightening and far too blatant a look at the reality of traumatic brain injury (TBI) and its aftermath.

"I can be there in a few hours," Phillip said insistently on the other end of the phone.

"Phillip, you just got home, and Katelyn needs to have a parent with her. She needs to be in school. We have no idea how long Rick is going to be here. I know that I need to be here with Rick right now. It has just been so hard today and I hate this place…..I hate everything about this place today," I continued to sob, as Phillip continued to provide the active listener ear that he has always provided.

"I am going to make some calls. I will talk to you again in a little while," he said. I could sense his frustration on the other end of the line. He verbalized feeling ineffective at work and felt isolated and helpless to address what was going on in Atlanta. He also acknowledged the importance of Katelyn being back at school. It was as hard for them to be in Aiken as it was for me to be in Atlanta.

Walking back into Rick's room, I saw him pulling and tugging on the wrist restraints.

"Get these things off of me. It's time for me to go to football practice," Rick insisted.

"Rick, you are in the hospital. I can take them off as long as I am with you, but you can't get up," I replied.

Removing one restraint, I waited for a few minutes to see how he would respond. Fumbling with the other, he tried his best to remove it, but he was unable to get his fingers to cooperate with the fine motor skill necessary for the task. Frustrated, his head fell back on the pillow and he looked at me for help. I knew that he could not get out of bed, even if he tried. Releasing the other restraint and putting the side rail down on the bed, I sat on the edge of Rick's bed.

"Did Dad get my football gear?" Rick asked.

"Rick, you don't play football. You are in the hospital. You wrecked your truck," I said ever-so quietly to him. He nodded his head and made no reply.

I sat like that for a while on the edge of Rick's bed, talking about his siblings and folks that had been praying for him at home. He lay there quietly, just listening. It was impossible to tell whether Rick comprehended what I was telling him. I tried to talk about regular things and regular people in his life, hoping that would help his memory. Maybe it was just helping me.

"Oh, Oh, Oh," he said suddenly. "I gotta poo!" he hollered, pointing to the bathroom door.

"Rick, you can't get up. You have a diaper on. It's ok." Looking at me with a blank expression on his face, that was that! I called the nurse, and together, we got Rick situated again.

"I'm sorry we have to do this, Rick," I said, as we rolled him over again.

"It's alright," he said, with a somewhat flat affect. "It ain't like you've never seen it before!" I laughed, totally knowing that I had just heard from the real Rick Lee. Amidst the heartbreaking task of changing the diaper on my 22-year-old son, God had given me yet another glimmer of hope at the end of a horribly long day.

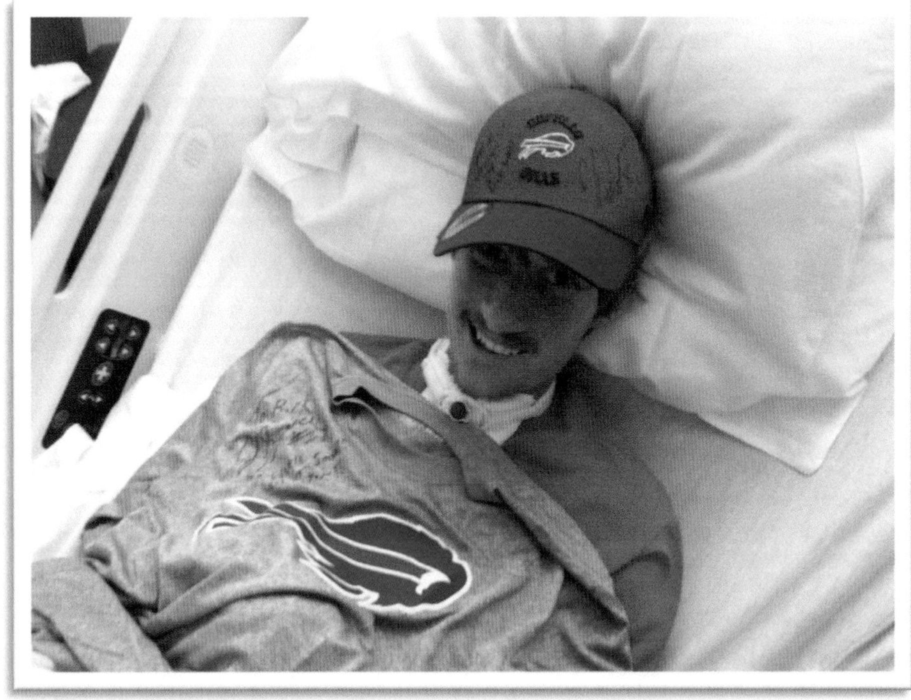

A personal gift with words of encouragement from C.J. Spiller (Clemson Tiger and Buffalo Bill Running Back)

Breath of Life

"The spirit of God made me and the breath of the Almighty gives me life."
Job 33:4(ESV)

Phillip and I talked for a long time on the phone that night. He was relieved to hear that my day had ended on a positive note and I was also relieved to hear how he and all of the other children were adjusting to being back at home, school, and work. We were all definitely trying to move forward, carrying out the things that each of us knew we needed to do. It was difficult on all of us to be apart but I believe that we all grew and gained strength in knowing that we were focused individually on what God called us to and purposed us for in that moment. And moment by moment is the only way we could manage it.

I was also relieved to hear that Phillip had talked to Wes and Keli that afternoon and that Keli was planning to come to Atlanta the next day. I was thankful to know that someone would be with me the next day as I continued to acclimate to the ABI unit.

Early the next morning, I went to the nurse manager's office, inquiring about the possibility of putting Rick in a private room. A semi-private room was the only room available when Rick was transferred out of ICU, but I was hoping and praying that status had changed. They placed Rick at the top of the list if a private room came open during the day. Returning to Rick's room, I found him once again struggling against the wrist restraints.

"Why am I tied up like a dog?" he asked disdainfully.

“We don’t want you to pull on any of the tubes,” I explained, loosening the ties and releasing his arms from the straps.

“I’m not gonna pull on anything,” he said, as he slipped his hands into his pants and started tugging on the catheter.

“Rick, hands on top of the covers, please!” I said, quickly pulling his hands away from the catheter.

“Devil woman,” he said under his breath.

“Rick, do you know where you are this morning?” I asked curiously.

“Texas,” he said without hesitation. Well, at least he’s in the right country now, I thought, smiling to myself.

“Rick, do you want to try some more ice chips this morning?” I asked, offering him the spoon as I spoke.

“Yea, maybe in a minute,” he answered, continuing to watch the TV in the corner of the room. I listened briefly to the announcer as he reported on a story from Dallas, Texas!
Oh Lord, help me today, I thought, putting the cup back on the bedside table.

Keli arrived around lunch-time and it was great to see her. Her company was a welcome presence in the room and Rick seemed to recognize her too, however, with little emotion. Rick typically had a very even temperament, but that seemed even more exacerbated since the accident.

The pulmonologist came in to see Rick and decided that it was time to discontinue the second chest tube. Removing the tape and gauze from around the tube, the physician assistant (PA) cut the sutures that held the chest tube in place. Instructing Rick to take a deep breath and blow out as hard as he could, the PA pulled the tube in one swift, continuous motion, quickly placing petroleum gauze over the opening where the chest tube had been. A portable chest x-ray was ordered to make sure that Rick’s lungs looked ok after the chest tube was pulled, but when the doctor came back in with the report, it was not the news that we wanted to hear.

"Rick's left lung shows evidence that air leaked back into the pleural space when the tube was pulled, causing a small area of the left lung to collapse again. I am going to put him on 100% non-rebreather mask for one hour and then do another portable chest x-ray. If the lung looks the same, we will keep him on the mask overnight and do another x-ray in the morning. If the lung looks worse, however, we will move him back to ICU in an hour and put the chest tube back in," the pulmonologist explained, waiting patiently for me to ask any questions.

"Ok, I understand," I replied, reaching for my phone to call Phillip. Explaining what the doctor had just said, I asked Phillip to send out an emergent email and blog, asking people to pray specifically for Rick and his lung situation over the next hour. Keli and I then joined hands and prayed fervently out in the hallway, begging God to protect Rick and heal his lungs. I was so thankful for my partner in prayer at that moment, but that would not be the only way that Keli would partner with me during her visit.

One hour later, the doctor came back and gave us great news. Rick's lung had stabilized and they would not need to put the chest tube back in.

"That's the power of prayer," I said emphatically to the pulmonologist, smiling from ear to ear.

"The power of prayer and 100% oxygen," replied the doctor.

For the next twenty-four hours, however, Rick would have to wear the oxygen mask over his face. This proved to be no simple task. I would put the mask over Rick's face, and then Rick would pull it off. Keli would put it back on, then Rick would pull it off. Over and over again, time after time. It was maddening. I went to the nurse's station again, inquiring about a private room.

"The pulmonologist says Rick needs to wear this mask all night. There is no way he is going to keep it on all night unless someone is in the room with him. I have already been told that I cannot stay in a semi-private room with Rick….So ya'll need to find a private room for us or plan to call security to have me removed tonight," I said seriously, but with as much southern, gentle quiet spirit as I was capable of at that time!

Rick was moved to a private room on the ABI unit within the next hour, still fighting to remove the face mask every five or ten minutes.

"Rick, do you want that chest tube put back in?" I asked directly.

He looked at me with a blank gaze on his face.

"Keep the mask on, Rick," I said firmly.

It stayed on for about five minutes, then he lifted his hand to remove it again. Catching his hand before he had a chance to reach the face mask, I gently put his hand back on his bed covers. I knew that he was not deliberately being cantankerous. He just wanted that mask off. It was irritating his eyes and nose and he wanted it off. His lungs depended on it though, so Keli and I knew clearly what our immediate role was to be.

We decided to take the night in shifts. I would keep watch over Rick for the first half while Keli tried to sleep at the apartment, then we would switch places. Neither of us slept much, but both of us kept that mask on Rick's face. The chest x-ray done the next morning showed that Rick's lung was completely re-inflated and the pulmonologist ordered that the face mask could come off.

It continues to amaze me, on a daily basis, how God richly supplies what and who we need moment by moment to get through the circumstances of life. We had no idea that those particular circumstances would unfold that day for Rick, but God knew, and he also knew that I needed help to make it through that night with Rick and that blessed face mask! Thank God for friends who are selfless, even on their birthday. And thank God for breathing that breath of life back into Rick's lungs. I know full-well where that 100% oxygen came from!

The Work Begins

"Lord, you know the hopes of the helpless. Surely you will hear their cries and comfort them."
Psalm 10:17

With both chest tubes out, it was much easier for the staff to get Rick ready for his first day of therapy. The process was still slow and Rick was very weak, having been primarily bedridden for nearly three weeks. There were periods of time that Rick seemed fairly oriented, but there were still episodes when he made no sense at all. Assisting the nurse technician with his bath, we finally had him dressed in sweat pants and a t-shirt, sitting in a wheelchair ready to go to the large rehabilitation room for breakfast. This was the first day that Rick would be integrated in with the other patients on the ABI unit for meals and group therapy, as well as individual intensive rehabilitation therapy. I was excited and very nervous at the same time. I had looked at the schedule for the day and knew that it was going to be long and laborious for Rick. After a complete evaluation with the rehabilitation doctor, Rick would be evaluated by speech therapy, occupational therapy, physical therapy, and recreational therapy. He would also be put through the rigors of a complete neurological-psychological evaluation to assess and monitor how he was responding and dealing with the entire aftermath of the accident and brain injury. It exhausted me just to look at the schedule, but I knew that it was all necessary and the very reason that we had been sent to Shepherd Center.

With the nurse tech pushing Rick's wheelchair, I was instructed to push the small suction machine close behind. Immediate suction had to be available for Rick at all times, just in case his trach became occluded with secretions, which required suctioning to clear the tube and allow Rick to breathe more easily.

Down the hall we paraded, finally entering the large room designated for therapy and patient meals. Positioning his wheelchair with a meal tray within reach, we sat patiently waiting on the meals to be served. A steady parade of patients and staff continued to enter the room, some with family members in attendance and some without. I suddenly realized that I felt hot and flushed, my heart pounding in my throat. I forced my attention to the clock on the wall, making every effort to fixate on the second-hand rather than on the other patients that were filing past Rick. The sudden deluge of sights and sounds of the other acquired brain injury patients was totally and completely devastating. The vast mirage of tragedy around me felt suffocating and obliterating. I stood quickly to reposition myself behind Rick's wheelchair, facing the wall. I did not want anyone to see the steady flow of tears that now rolled down my cheeks.

Gulping for air and praying myself back into focus, I realized that this was the first exposure Rick was having to the overall atmosphere of the ABI Unit. Walking back around to face him, I knelt down beside his chair and took his hand.

"Rick, are you feeling ok? We are just waiting on your meal to come," I said, trying to reassure both of us as I spoke.

"Yea," he said flatly. "I want to go back to bed." Resting his head on his hand, he slumped down in the wheelchair as much as the posey vest that had him tied in would allow. He occasionally glanced around the room at the other patients, but other than that, sat emotionless in his wheelchair.

The breakfast trays finally came and the room became a buzz of activity. Sitting the tray in front of Rick, I opened all of the containers and set the utensils within easy reach.

"Encourage him to do it," one of the therapists instructed, walking by as she smiled at Rick and me. I nodded nervously and pulled up a chair so that I could sit facing Rick.

"Ok, Rick. It's time to eat," I said.

Looking blankly at me, he looked down at the tray and remained otherwise motionless. The occupational therapist was watching the scenario unfold so I made no move to assist.

"Rick, pick up your fork and take a bite of eggs for me," she said.

He looked at the tray again and made no effort to move. Picking up the fork, the therapist placed the utensil in Rick's hand and helped him curl his fingers around it. Awkwardly attempting to coax eggs onto the end of the fork, Rick began raising the food to his mouth, only to have it end up down the front of his shirt and in his lap. After thirty minutes of prompting, he had managed to eat two bites of eggs, a bite of pancake, and had taken a sip of apple juice. Announcing that he was finished, he slumped down in the wheelchair, resting his head on his hand. I wondered if being in the general assembly type-room was bothering Rick. There was absolutely no way for me to know.

The room continued in its bustle as patients finished their meal and moved into the morning schedule of therapy. Rick was scheduled to attend his first session of psych therapy, a group therapy session where patients were given the opportunity to express feelings or begin talking about their injuries and hospitalization. I was scheduled to attend the first of several mandatory meetings regarding Rick's potential disability and hospital billing details. Reluctantly, I left Rick sitting in a room with a therapist and one other patient that was continually screaming arbitrary profanities at the wall. Sadly, I felt like I could identify with that patient's state of mind.

Navigating my way through the hospital, I finally found the Disability Administration Office on one of the top floors. Knocking on the door, I was quickly summoned to enter, and there, sitting behind the desk, was a man in a wheelchair. After an hour of talking, filling out paperwork, and conference calls back and forth with Philip, the official portion of the meeting ended. Having sensed my occasional attempts to evade some of the questions during the meeting, the gentleman finally put the pen and paperwork away and began to talk.

"Filling out all of this stuff doesn't mean that your son is going to be disabled. We just always initiate the process so that things are not delayed down the road if he does need assistance. He will be automatically re-evaluated in ninety days to see if he does qualify for anything," he said, pausing briefly to see if I had any more questions. I left the room feeling a little dazed.

Meanwhile, Rick was back in psych therapy listening to the therapist explain why they were there. "You are at Shepherd Center, a hospital that specializes in brain and spinal cord injuries," she continued, allowing time for all of the patients to respond. By the time I got back to the ABI Unit, Rick was back in his room lying in the bed.

"How was it, Rick?" I asked.

"Which one am I?" he asked quietly.

"What are you talking about, buddy?"

"I have been laying here in the bed since I got back from that meeting: She said it's a brain and spinal cord place. I can move my legs. I'm not paralyzed. What's wrong with me?" he asked.

That was the first totally lucid moment that Rick had exhibited since the accident. His gaze did not leave mine as I slowly lowered the side rail on his bed and sat down beside him. Starting at the beginning, I slowly told Rick, as simply as I could, what had transpired over the past several weeks.

"I want to go home," Rick said slowly, blinking his eyes several times as he looked away.

"Rick you are getting better every day. It's just going to take some time," I replied quietly.

We sat in silence for a little while. I could not even begin to imagine how Rick was feeling or what was going through his mind. He lifted his T-shirt and ran his hand up and down the tube that was inserted into his stomach.

"What's this thing for?" he asked, pulling slightly at the tape surrounding the tube.

Moving his hand quickly away from the tube, I explained that he was being fed liquid nutrition through the tube until he was able to take in enough calories by mouth on his own.

"You need extra calories for healing, Rick, and you have also lost weight since the accident. You need the energy that the extra calories will provide in order to do your rehabilitation every day."

"I want to go home," he said again, this time with obvious frustration.

"I know. I do too. So we are gonna work hard every day. Do exactly what the therapists say. And we will go home together, Rick."

Laying his head back on the pillow, he stared silently at the television set, attempting to process our conversation.

"I feel fine," he said emphatically. The only thing that's bothering me is the stuff they did to me," pointing to his feeding tube and to his trach. "<u>THEY</u> messed me up," Rick concluded abruptly.

"Rick, these things, and all that the hospitals have done, have helped to save your life. You could not breathe on your own. All that has been done was completely necessary. You know that. I know that it is frustrating to have this stuff….to be in this place…..but you <u>ARE</u> getting better…..you will not have these tubes forever, Rick. YOU ARE GETTING BETTER EVERY DAY," I said lovingly but firmly.

"I want to go home," he repeated again, looking directly at me and blinking hard as he spoke. I had seen that look on my little boy's face so many times and I knew exactly what was about to happen. Sliding a little closer to Rick, I took his hand in mine and rubbed it gently.

"Rick, do you want to cry? It's ok to cry," I said in a whisper.

I suppose that's all either of us needed. Sitting in silence, tears quickly began to roll over the little red freckles on Rick's face. Closing my eyes for a moment, I envisioned the old brown rocking chair again that sat at home. That's what I'm doing right now, I thought. I am rocking one of my precious babies.

POINTS TO PONDER

- **In what ways has God provided people in your life at just the right time? Are you resistant to receiving assistance from others when you are at the end of your rope or are in crisis?**

- **What is your typical response to feeling overwhelmed or in overload?**

- **Do you feel that expressing emotions openly and honestly is wrong? Helpful? Are you often times resistant or do you have difficulty being transparent with other people when you are hurting?**

A New Work

"For I am about to do something new. See, I have already begun! Do you not see it? I will make a pathway through the wilderness, I will create rivers in the dry wasteland."
Isaiah 43:19

Phillip, Misty, and the children came back and forth to Atlanta on the weekends and that was a huge bright spot for Rick and me. College football is huge at the Lee house and we incorporated that tradition right into our time at Shepherd Center. Rebecca and Ben had also come from Anderson, so we captured the moment to celebrate some family time surrounding a large screen TV in one of the therapy rooms. A little Clemson football and the sound of "Tiger Rag" was just what the doctor had ordered! Medicinal…..purely medicinal!!

With so many people sleeping in the single room apartment, we secured a hotel room for Phillip and me and for Rebecca for that night. We were only about a mile from the hospital, but it was a breath of fresh air to be out of the hospital for a little while. Phillip and I also had so much to talk about…..the other children…..things at church…..finances at home and finances in Atlanta….and finally, each other. We had been talking on the phone several times a day, but there was no substitution for finally being together.

The weekend passed way too quickly, and before we knew it, Rick and I were back in the middle of his rehab sessions. The days were long and exhausting for him. Occupational therapy would start the day very early, which was an automatic aggravation for Rick. Placing a gate belt, or walking belt, around his waist, we hoisted him into a standing position. Allowing him a minute or so to get his balance, we slowly assisted him in turning towards the bathroom. Guiding him slowly into the bathroom, he paused and looked at his reflection in the mirror. Slowly and with great effort, he raised his right arm, rubbing his hand on the large bald spot that still remained on the right side of his head. Then looking at his trach, he said slowly and with very little emotion, "They messed me up."

Sitting him on a bathing chair, the occupational therapist began an arduous process of re-training Rick on how to do his morning toiletry activities. Bridled in the corner of the room, it was so difficult for me to watch Rick attempt to get toothpaste on the toothbrush. Once the task was finally accomplished, he had no idea what to do with the object.

"What do you need to do now, Rick?" asked the therapist.

Shrugging his shoulders, Rick sat in the chair gazing at the floor. Taking the toothbrush in her hand, the therapist told Rick to open his mouth. His facial expressions were still very lop-sided and this made brushing his teeth quite a challenge. As the toothbrush went in, Rick clenched his teeth and bit down hard on the toothbrush. Finally coaxing him to open his mouth again, the therapist and I both made a mental note to refrain from putting our fingers in Rick's mouth! Finally coming out of the bathroom, he caught a glimpse of his camouflage hat sitting on the table. Pointing to the hat, he motioned for me to hand it to him as he inched his way towards the wheelchair. Once in his hand, he popped it onto his head with ease. Humm…..I thought………I bet he knows what to do with that toothbrush!

Physical therapy, speech therapy, and neuropsychology group therapy also had to be completed every day. Rick had very little energy and even less stamina during the therapy sessions and each therapist would spend a portion of each day encouraging him to work hard and not give up. Not being allowed to sit in on the group therapy sessions, I usually sat in Rick's room or did laundry during that time. Once Rick had completed the group session, the therapy assistant would bring Rick back to the room and allow him to rest for a while.

“Rick, how was your group session? What did ya’ll talk about?” I asked curiously.

“One of the other guys asked me if I’ve ever seen boobs,” Rick said very matter-of-factly.

Trying to smother my laughter, I asked calmly, “Really! What did you say?”

Easing the blankets up and pulling his hat down over his eyes, he made no move to reply….and I decided that it was prudent to probe no further!

Two more weeks of intensive rehabilitation therapy passed and Rick was improving every day. The tasks were often repetitious but had a defined purpose in each session. He had gone from only being able to walk a few steps to being able to walk down the hallway to the therapy room. He continued to have a great amount of difficulty with fine motor movement in his hands. He would sit for long periods of time each day attempting to place little round pegs on a wooden board, a task that usually led him to use words that he had probably learned from his mother! His thought processes were becoming more and more clear, but he was continuing to have difficulty with his emotional responses to people. With the exception of several episodes of crying during the first week or two at Shepherd Center, Rick was fairly “emotionless.” Misty had been to see him several times and we had been surprised at his lack of response to her and to others as they came to visit. A meeting with Rick’s rehab doctor and case manager helped us understand what we were seeing in Rick that week.

“There are three classifications of brain injuries,” the doctor began to explain. “Mild….moderate….and severe…. Rick has sustained a severe brain injury, primarily to the frontal lobe portion of his brain. That means there is a chance that he may never respond appropriately, or what you are accustomed to seeing in Rick, from an emotional stand-point. He may also have trouble recognizing the emotions of other people. He will, more than likely, need help planning and scheduling his day and it is doubtful that he will be able to return to a completely independent level of functioning or living."

Phillip and I glanced nervously at one another. I was trying desperately to digest the information that we had just been given, but suddenly realized that my mouth was completely dry and I felt a little queasy.

"He is a youth pastor and also works at an outdoor store," Phillip said evenly. "Are you telling us that he will not be able to go back to work?"

"He may be able to work at the outdoor store," the doctor continued. "But he may have difficulty in the role of a pastor. Again, he may not respond appropriately or recognize others' emotions due to the severity and location of his injury. We have decided, however, that he will be ready for outpatient rehabilitation much earlier than we had anticipated. The out-patient therapy will still be Monday through Friday for another eight weeks, possibly, once he is discharged as an inpatient. Do you have any other questions?" he concluded.

Fumbling through several other general questions, the meeting was adjourned and we were left standing in the empty room.

"What are we supposed to tell Rick?" I asked Phillip, searching his face for comfort and wisdom.

"We will tell him the truth," Phillip answered, without hesitation.

Going back to Rick's room I sat and listened as Phillip explained the information to him. The father was talking but the pastor was present. I was once again amazed and so thankful for my husband.

"Rick, you are getting better every day, even faster than they thought you would. We will be with you every step of the way. We will take one day at the time and we are going to trust the call that God placed on your life. Remember what Beau told us. This is all just going to be part of your story."

"When can I go hunting?" Rick asked, un-phased by the other information.

"I don't know about that, Rick," I replied, pointing to his still-deformed protruding left collar bone.

"I will learn to shoot right-handed," Rick replied flatly. "Line those doctors up. I bet they won't come in here if I am holding a gun!" he said confidently and with definite emotion.

"We'll see, Rick. We'll see," Phillip said, with a smile on his face.

Rick continued to break all speed limits with his inpatient therapy. His strength was slowly returning but his appetite and fine motor skills in his hands were both still lagging behind. He continued to struggle a bit with feeding himself and would often want to give up the attempts far before he had taken in enough calories. Reminding myself that Rick had also been gifted with an extra "lazy gene" at birth, I found myself getting cantankerous with him.

"Eat, Rick, or they will never be able to pull that feeding tube out. You look like a refugee," I teased, as I slid the plate a little closer to him.

"Maybe in a minute," he answered, watching ESPN calmly.

"Rick, take three more bites then we are going to walk around to the nurse's station and see how much you weigh," I said insistently.

Two more bites were accomplished. Sliding the gait belt around Rick's waist, we walked slowly down the hall and around the corner to the scales.

"You hop up there first," Rick said, his facial expression never changing.

"Kiss my rear end, Rick," I said, laughing as I zeroed the scale. I had no difficultly with my appetite!

Rick stood at a tall 6'2" and weighed in at a whopping 136 pounds that day.

"Rick, if I have to sit you in a corner and feed you with a sling-shot, then that's what I am gonna do!" I proclaimed.

The long days of therapy continued. Rick had to learn every aspect of daily living again….everything from bathing and dressing in the morning to learning how to interact with others in the day room. The therapists were always watching. He was allowed to go on several outings with two other patients and an entourage of therapists. They spent time walking on the sidewalk in front of Shepherd Center and spent day after day learning to cross the street again. If you can learn to do that in Atlanta then I say you are ready for discharge!

The next day, the pulmonologist came in and gave us news that we had been anxious to hear. Rick's trach tube was discontinued that morning and was replaced by a big bulky dressing, which would require changing twice a day. Finally, almost four weeks after the accident, that tube was pulled and the opening would slowly begin to close on its own. I felt relief, amazement, and a vast amount of thankfulness as I watched the respiratory therapist remove the tube. That night, as I opened my Bible to read aloud to him before going to sleep, I was overpowered with the definite sense that God really was making all things new with Rick. I could see it!

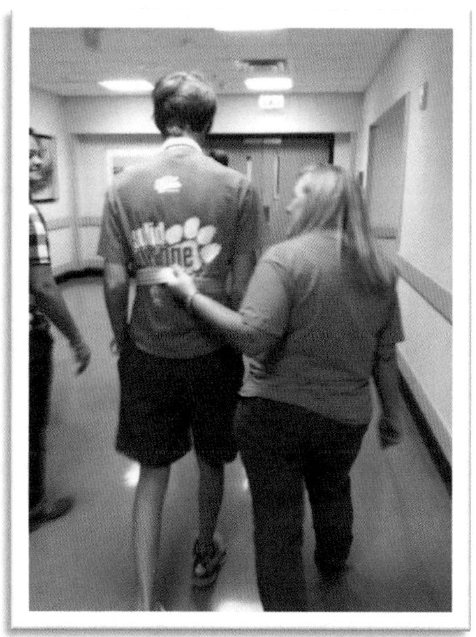

Up and walking!

Clemson Game Day…A Lee family tradition

Moving Day…Again!

"For God is working in you, giving you the desire and the power to do what pleases him."
Philippians 2:13

It was moving day! Rick was finally being released as an inpatient from Shepherd Center. His feeding tube had been removed and he was given permission to eat and drink whatever he wanted to, with the exception of alcohol and caffeine, which were both off limits during the first full year of recovery due to the increased risk of seizures. Phillip, Rick and I walked slowly through the doors of the Acquired Brain Injury Unit. His entire team of nurses and therapists stood behind, waving and crying as we moved towards the elevator. We had been there for over a month and this place that had once been so frightening and depressing to me now had an irreplaceable place in my heart. Our family realized that, while the stories may be tragic and depressing, Shepherd Center was a place of hope and healing in so many different ways.

We walked Rick over to the apartment that had become our home away from home. I had already placed pictures of his youth group, our family, Misty, and Chipper strategically around the room. His favorite hunting hat and container of Oreo Double-Stuff cookies sat on the kitchen table. I began to cry as I was acutely reminded that home has nothing to do with location or size, but yet the precious presence of those that you hold dear. Orienting Rick to his new surroundings, Phillip and I sat quietly as we watched him meander around the room. Finally settling into the chair across from the kitchen table, he was content to channel surf on the small TV while Phillip and I put some things away.

We spent the rest of that weekend wandering around Atlanta. Rick was to begin outpatient intensive therapy on Monday morning and I needed to be able to find my way to the outpatient facility. Driving in Atlanta was not something that this country girl looked forward to! We made the short trip back and forth from the apartment to the outpatient facility several times that weekend and I finally became comfortable with the route. I was being stretched and forced to grow in every possible area of my life. We all were.

Phillip left Saturday evening in order to get back for the church services the next morning. We stood for a long time at the car, just holding each other. The estimated eight weeks of outpatient therapy loomed in front of us like a dark cloud. We were thankful to be where we were, but were also continuing to deal with the stress and fatigue that we were all feeling. Rick still had so much rehabilitation to do and there were still so many questions regarding what his level of independence would be when outpatient therapy was complete. We were forced to stay focused on one day at a time and trust that God continued to have a plan and purpose in all of it.

Monday morning arrived quickly and I was a little anxious about my first day of caring for Rick completely on my own. Waking up early, I showered and dressed quickly so that I could wake him up and begin his morning routine. Nudging him gently, I held out his medication and a small glass of water. Rick had been placed on a medication called "Amantadine" which is typically used in the treatment of Parkinson's disease. This drug also has a stimulant-type effect and is used with traumatic brain injury patients in an effort to "wake-up" the brain. The neurologist explained that it was similar to giving Rick's brain several cups of coffee and that it has been useful in traumatic brain injury recovery when given during the first several months following the injury. I administered the medication and then began to organize the supplies that I needed to perform Rick's trach site dressing change. Covering the opening in Rick's neck with an occlusive dressing, I led him into the shower to make sure he was able to get the water temperature set just right. Once I was satisfied that he was safely attending to himself, I gave him privacy to complete the task so that I could get his breakfast ready.

Rick was notorious for staying in the shower at home until every bit of the hot water was gone! We often teased him about the time that he had fallen asleep in the shower pulling the entire shower curtain down around him as he fell! It's amazing that this was his first head injury!

"Rick, you awake?" I asked teasingly, as I poked my head into the bathroom. "Get a move on!" I hollered, as I closed the door to let him finish his shower.

Emerging from the bathroom about ten minutes later, he slowly fumbled with his clothes trying several times to button his shirt. The motor movement deficits in his fingers still would not allow him to complete this task.

"Rick, can I help you?" I asked carefully. He allowed his hands to drop to his side as I reached to button his shirt.

"I am going to change the dressing on your trach site now Rick. It won't take long. Then you can eat."

I carefully pulled the tape loose and removed the dressing from Rick's neck. The outer opening was approximately the size of a nickel but the innermost part of the tissue was beginning to close nicely. He coughed suddenly and a small plug of mucous flew from the opening.

"That's good, Rick. That's good for your lungs."

Finishing the dressing change, Rick poked at my neck as I poked at his. He was acting more and more like "the old Rick" every day.

Pulling the car out of the parking garage, I turned onto Peachtree Road and into the Atlanta morning traffic. I felt a sudden sense of strength and confidence as our car was quickly engulfed in the early morning frenzy of people trying to get to work. I can do this, I thought. We can do this, Rick! Arriving at the outpatient facility about fifteen minutes early, Rick and I sat patiently in the waiting room. The lobby began to fill as other patients and family members arrived. I was, yet again, unprepared for the continual parade of wheelchair-dependent and brain-injured people as they were pushed or filed by. I reached over and took Rick's hand as we sat bathing once again in the reality of our circumstances. My heart hurt as I recognized the fact that there were so many that obviously had much more rehab ahead of them than Rick did. I was not able to coax myself to make eye contact with any of the other mothers. Not on that day.

We were eventually called to the case manager's office and our first day of outpatient intensive therapy began. We slowly toured the entire facility and were introduced to Rick's team of caregivers: physical therapists, an occupational therapist, a speech therapist, a recreational therapist, a new rehabilitation physician, two neuropsychologists, and a mental health counselor. We concluded the tour in a room that housed the driving simulator, a machine that Rick would eventually use to learn how to drive again. I looked at the case manager incredulously as she explained how the machine worked.

"The occupational therapist will decide if and when Rick is ready for this," she explained carefully, recognizing the horrified look on my face.

"I'm ready now," Rick said frankly.

"Your mother is not ready for this," I replied promptly.

Realizing that she had opened a can of worms before it was time to go fishing; the case manager eased us out of the room and down the hallway. Back in her office, the case manager continued to explain that Rick would undergo a massive amount of physical and neuropsychological evaluations in the days to come. Therapy was scheduled Monday through Friday from eleven to four, for a six to eight week duration.

"The team will meet and evaluate his overall progress at the end of each week," the case manager continued. "Our goal is to return Rick to the highest level of independent living possible."

"When can I go hunting?" Rick asked abruptly.

The case manager looked at Rick and me, shuffling nervously through a stack of papers.

"We will need to talk to the doctor about that," she replied, avoiding the question all together. I knew that would not suffice for Rick.

We talked about hunting all the way back to the apartment that day. I stopped by the bookstore and picked up a few hunting and fishing magazines for Rick to look at in the evenings, thinking that would help. In some ways, I think it only increased his frustration.

"Let that frustration be your drive. Work hard every day in your therapy sessions," I encouraged. "The surest way not to fail is to determine to succeed."

I enjoyed fixing Rick's supper that night. We had picked up a few of his favorite things at the grocery store and he appeared to be enjoying the taste of food again. He ate slowly and methodically, reminding me so much of my dad, as he took his sweet time in finishing everything on his plate. With food across his face and down the front of his shirt, I pushed the napkin towards him, winking at him as I got up to clear the table. After supper, we walked over to one of the family rooms and sat down together at the computer.

"Let's watch Dad's sermon from yesterday, Rick," I said excitedly, typing in the address to the Cedar Creek Church web-site.

"These last several weeks have really reminded me of how important it is to have our lives built on a solid foundation that can withstand the storms of life," Phillip began. "There is no firmer foundation than the unchanging truth and promises of scripture. I can't tell you the number of nights over the past month that our family has left the hospital feeling drained, discouraged and unsure of the future. But each night as we gathered in the hotel room or apartment and opened God's Word together, we literally felt God breathing His strength, hope and encouragement into us. I have a renewed desire and hunger for

The Word like never before and I want you to experience that in your life as well."

THAT is the reason I am in Atlanta and Phillip is in Aiken, I thought. I was so proud of him.

"I love that man, Rick" I said, smiling and nodding at the computer.

Rick shook his head and kept staring at the computer.

I talked to Phillip for a while on the phone while Rick talked to Misty, then we walked up to sit on the roof. We sat in silence for a long time, just staring at the traffic as it crawled by far below. We watched as a rescue helicopter circled the hospital, and then slowly disappeared around the corner into the darkness of night. I shivered, though not from the cold, as I thought about Rick being in one of those helicopters.

"What did you think of your first day in outpatient therapy, Rick?" I asked, intentionally choosing to direct my thoughts elsewhere.

"It was ok. I'm ready to go home," he replied flatly.

So, on Friday, that's exactly what we did! The rehabilitation doctor had given us permission to take Rick home so that he could escort Katelyn for homecoming at Aiken High School. We were all so excited and anticipatory of our own first "homecoming" since the night of the accident. Stopping briefly to grab something to eat on our way home, we finally turned the car towards Aiken and headed for the barn. I could barely contain my excitement as we drove onto our street. Samantha, a dear friend and Rick's favorite "hair cutter", had agreed to meet us at the house. A peach-fuzz of new hair growth covered one side of Rick's head, and the other side was covered with his typical red strands of hair. Samantha's task was to "even things up" as much as she could! She did a great job, especially taking into account that she wore a Clemson football jersey over to the house!! What a precious gesture for that die-hard Carolina Gamecock!

Phillip helped Rick into the shower and then helped him get into his suit. The sport coat seemed to swallow him whole as we wrapped it around his thin frame. He had never looked more handsome.

Arriving early, we pulled right up to the gate so that Rick would not have as far to walk. Escorting Katelyn onto the field, the stadium erupted with cheers and clapping as Katelyn and Rick's names were announced. <u>This</u> is what is marking Katelyn's senior year in high school, I thought, sobbing as I watched them both walk across the field. Katelyn was not crowned homecoming queen that night at Aiken High School, but I am pretty sure that she would say it was the best homecoming ever.

God's Call

"But even before I was born, God chose me and called me by his marvelous grace. Then it pleased him to reveal His Son to me so that I would proclaim the Good News about Jesus to the Gentiles."
Galatians 1:15-16

Sunday seemed to come before we could blink an eye. It was time for Rick and me to head back to Atlanta. I was really nervous about driving back into the Atlanta traffic and about being able to get us back to the apartment at Shepherd Center. Phillip had been over and over the instructions with me, so without further delay, we loaded the car and headed for Georgia's capital city. As we entered the thickest part of the swiftly moving traffic, I chuckled to myself and gripped the steering wheel a little tighter.

"Ok, Rick. I'm gonna use my brain to drive but I need your eyes! Follow Dad's directions and tell me where my exits are!"

Finally pulling into the parking garage at Shepherd Center, I shoved the car into "park" and let out a sigh of relief.

"Holy cow, we made it, Rick! Praise the Lord and pass me some chocolate!!!"

"You're brain injured," Rick said, shaking his head as he tossed me a Reese's cup.

Calling Phillip to let him know that we had arrived safely, we quickly unloaded the car and began to get ready for another week of outpatient therapy. Changing the dressing on Rick's trach site, I systematically laid out his medication and supplies for the next morning. I was growing very accustomed to the routine and knew exactly how much time to allow for every part of Rick's care. His thought processes were clear and coherent, but he could not always get the motor responses that he was expecting with his arms and legs. Extra time always had to be allowed for activities that require fine motor movement with his hands. Tying his shoes was a completely frustrating task so we opted for slip-on shoes most of the time.

One week passed into another, and before we knew it, the occupational therapist began talking to Rick about getting into the driving simulator. Explaining that they would just be "testing Rick's reflexes" to begin with, they disappeared into "the room." I was furious.

Meandering down the hallway, divine intervention would once again occur and I just happened to run into the rehabilitation psychologist. Reading the expression on my face, she motioned to her empty office, offering me a safe haven for the emotional explosion that she accurately sensed was imminent.

"He's not ready for this," I screamed. "He can't button his own shirt! He's not ready." I searched her face in earnest, waiting for her to validate my thoughts.

"He will be ready before you are," she replied quietly, taking my hands in hers as she sat facing me.

"I am afraid," I admitted softly. "I am so damn afraid."

And then I wept. For the longest time, I just wept. She never really said anything that was earth-shattering… no huge words of wisdom that made everything better. She was just an ever-present active listener. She was just there. Rick and I both received outpatient intensive therapy that day.

I began to get to know some of the other families that were also a part of Shepherd Center. As we shared the stories of what had led us there, we began to gain strength and encouragement from one another. It also helped me be more intentional and specific about how to pray for the other families and patients. I was amazed to hear that some of the folks had a ten or twelve hour drive on the weekends, as they came back and forth to visit like Phillip and the children were doing. I began to share some of the meal and gas gift cards that our Cedar Creek

Church family had given us, hoping that this would help to lighten their financial load as it had done for us.

All of the therapists were beginning to get to know Rick on a more personal level too. They asked him detailed questions about his work and about his hobbies. The recreational therapist even brought in a golden retriever for Rick to interact with during one of his sessions. He "worked" with the dog for two hours that afternoon and it was the best therapy that Rick could havc had.

His face lit up as he talked about his youth group back at Cedar Creek Church on the Ridge. He talked about Sunday evening youth services and about his role as a youth pastor.

"Rick, I want you to write a sermon for me," the speech therapist said. "I want you to create an outline…. Do it just like you would do it if you were at home. Then next week, I want you to preach for us. Do you think you can do that?" she concluded.

"Yep," Rick replied, without hesitation and with a smile on his face.

For the next several nights, I watched Rick work on that outline. With his Bible in front of him and a notepad on his lap, he strained to curl his fingers around the pen in his hand. But he never put the pen down. The handwriting was completely illegible at times, but Rick knew what it said. He knew exactly what it said because he knew exactly what God had called him to do. The next week, Rick sat in a room filled with his outpatient therapy team…. and the post-traumatic brain injured Rick Lee delivered his sermon.

"Jesus is real and Jesus is relevant." Rick said decidedly. "No matter what our circumstances are, He is there and He is working in it. And I have a job….a job to make Him known," Rick paused for a minute, looking around at the room. "I know that's what I'm supposed to do. And I know it doesn't depend on my brain. It depends on Jesus."

Word!! Amen brother! Preach it, preacher! I believe with all my heart that Rick knew at that moment, beyond a shadow of a doubt, that he was going to be fine. He knew that he still had some areas of recovery, but I believe that he knew that he was going to be 100% restored in order to continue his calling as a youth pastor. His confidence was not in himself or in his ability to do anything. His confidence was in Jesus.

I laid awake for a long time that night thinking about Rick's sermon. I also thought about the apostle Paul….how he had preached the Good News even in prison. Rick had "loosened the chains" of rehab that day, proclaiming that God's call on his life had not changed, despite his present circumstances and his confinement in a rehabilitation facility. It was evident that day that Rick Lee was not confined at all.

Preach it preacher!

POINTS TO PONDER

- **Have you ever felt that God has used you at an unpredictable time or in an unusual situation?**

- **How might God use you in your everyday life to impact others? What people or opportunities is God placing in your path? If possible, be specific with names and commit to pray for and encourage these people daily.**

God is Good

"And we know that God causes everything to work together for the good of those who love God and are called according to his purpose for them."
Romans 8:28

The next several weeks seemed to drag by. Rick spent six hours a day in therapy. He worked very hard, doing exactly what the therapists asked him to do. He saw purpose in some of the activities, but also became very frustrated with some of the sessions. He continued to work on balance, coordination and other therapies that assisted him in building his endurance. I continued to spend time talking with other families and also learned my way up and down the road right in front of the out-patient facility. I found Target and Chick-fil-A. What else does a girl need!! I also talked on the phone in the afternoons. My conversations with Cindy and Anita were a great source of strength and encouragement for me as I began to think about taking Rick home. He had progressed much farther than anyone had anticipated that he would, and before we knew it, the team announced that they thought Rick was approaching discharge.

"We know that Rick has only been in outpatient intensive therapy for about 4 weeks," his case manager said. "The entire therapy team believes that Rick is ready for discharge."

"What does that mean?" I asked carefully. "Rick can go home?"

"He is not able to return to independent living yet. The therapy team is recommending discharge home with family for now. You will need to continue to change his trach site dressing twice a day until it has healed completely. All family members and friends that will be with Rick also need to be educated on what to do if Rick has a seizure. Rick will always be at greater risk of having seizures now."

"When can I go back to my place?" Rick asked. "And I want to go hunting, too. When can I do what I want to do?" he asked directly.

"You will need to stay with your family until the beginning of the year, Rick. In the meantime, you will be scheduled to come back to Shepherd Center in approximately two weeks. At that time, you will undergo an extensive six hour neurological and psychological evaluation. If the rehabilitation team is satisfied with the results of that evaluation, then you may take your driver's test again and you will be cleared for independent living. How does that sound?"

"I'm gonna be driving and duck hunting by New Year's Day," Rick said decidedly, standing to leave the room as he placed his camouflage hat on top of his head.

"See you in two weeks," she said, smiling and nodding at both of us as we left the room.

Packing up the car and cleaning the apartment for the last time, I turned and looked around the now barren room that had been our home for almost two months. I was caught off guard by the wide array of emotions that I was feeling. I was so happy….overjoyed to be going home….yet I felt sadness too. I thought about the patients and families that we had met as inpatients…. and the patients and families that I knew would continue to be at Shepherd Center through the upcoming holidays. I felt grief and guilt when I thought about the blessings that we had received compared to so many that continued to be in pain and suffering. The faces of several of the other mothers that I had gotten to know passed through my mind as I closed the door to the apartment. God, be with them, I whispered, as Rick and I turned towards the car.

I smiled to myself as I eased the car out into the afternoon Atlanta traffic, loosely holding the steering wheel. "We've got this, don't we Rick!" I said confidently. God's strength had been present in every moment of my weakness and doubt. I had grown to enjoy the frenzy of the city.

Rick talked constantly all the way home. He had totally lost about six weeks of his memory, not remembering anything at all from the night of the accident until mid-October. He asked question after question, and then would start all over again, asking the same questions as though we had never discussed anything. It was humorous and maddening at the same time. I was mentally and physically exhausted when we drove up in our driveway. Phillip and all the children came out to greet us. It was an unbelievable moment in the life of our family and one that we will never forget.

We all sat in the den for several hours, just watching TV and laughing at anything and everything. Rick continued to ask questions and we all took turns answering over and over again. In many ways, it was like watching a computer re-boot!
I did seizure precaution education with anyone that remotely looked at Rick. I was tempted to do the training with the mailman one afternoon as I saw him dropping the mail off! It did not take me long to realize that I was having some trouble readjusting to normal life after Rick's traumatic brain injury.

Everyone seemed to be back to life as usual. I had trouble sleeping, could not relax, felt depressed, and cried on and off almost every day. I went to church and felt totally isolated. "I'm not ok!" I wanted to scream. Ugh, what is the matter with me, I thought?? I am so not ok.

Days passed, and Rick and I headed back to Atlanta one last time for his final evaluation. I knew that we would possibly have the results in several weeks and that meant Rick may be released to go back to his own home. I knew that I was holding him too tightly. I began meeting with Dr. Gary Powell, our church counselor, for one hour once a week. All I had to do was put the car in drive and head towards the church. The tears started flowing every time, well before my arrival for the sessions with Gary. The sessions were precious to me and Gary is a pro at what he does. He is one of the most calming and caring people that I have ever met.

Gary got me to start at the very beginning of the story…. not on the night of Rick's accident…. but on the day of my parents' accident….on the day of my parents' death. There was something very healing and very cathartic about going back to the very beginning of my story. I began to understand things about myself….about my personality… about my parenting…. why I am the way that I am….and finally began to understand that God does cause everything to work together for good.

My mother was a strong disciplinarian and for years I had resented her for that. In the years following her death, however, I realized that her discipline and drive for us to succeed was what prepared me for life without parents at the age of seventeen. I now love and respect her for instilling in me a drive for excellence and a determination to succeed as a wife, mother, and nurse. The pain of the loss of my parents also gave me an earnest determination to have with my children what I was never able to have with my parents due to their untimely death…. a strong, involved, intimate relationship with my kids. I longed for there to be a perfect mix of love and discipline. And I guess, above all, I did not want to ever lose one of them. I did not want for anything bad to happen again. I did not want to ever feel pain like that again and I did not want them to hurt either.

So, I finally realized that I had become a controller…. an angry, fearful, controller. I parented from a posture of anger and fear. I was angry when I could not reach them on the phone. I was angry when I did not have every single detail or fact about where they were or what they were doing. I was angry because I was fearful.

Then on September 4, nearly thirty-three years after the first accident that forever changed my life, there was a second accident. My sense of control and protection over my children evaporated like rain on a hot summer day. It had been nothing more than years of my own attempt to be God.

As I stood in Rick's hospital room at Palmetto Richland Hospital, I finally stopped parenting from a posture of fear and decided to parent from a posture of faith. I surrendered. I finally fully surrendered Phillip and my children to God....and I surrendered my control.... or lack of control.... to God. I cried out desperately for God that day. I cried out to Him in a way I have never cried before. I finally acknowledged and trusted that He really does have a purpose and plan for each of us and that His ways are so much better than our ways, even when we don't understand them. I again casted every single worry and care that I had on him and finally, for the first time since my parents' death, felt total peace.

I still don't fully understand why my parents died and Rick lived. I believe that there are some things that we will never understand this side of heaven. But I do know, now more than ever, that God uses every situation for good. Everything is not good, but he causes everything to work together for good. He simply wants us to desperately acknowledge Him and to surrender to Him every aspect of our lives, to cast all our cares on Him, and to trust that He has a plan and purpose in everything.

Rick eventually passed all evaluations with flying colors. Phillip took him to a rehabilitation facility in Greenville, South Carolina at the end of the year and he passed a four hour extensive driving evaluation with no difficulty whatsoever. He has no feeling in two fingers on his left hand, some residual hearing loss in the left ear, and scars from the many lines and tubes that helped to sustain his life. He occasionally says things that are inappropriate, but don't we all!!

In late December 2012, Rick Lee bought another truck, and the first week of January 2013, he and his dad left to go on a week-long duck hunting trip in the Mississippi Delta.

Rick is currently serving as the youth pastor at Cedar Creek Church on the Ridge, and had the recent privilege to participate in the baptism of forty-seven young people during summer camp.

"'For I know the plans I have for you,' says the Lord. 'They are plans for good and not for disaster, to give you a future and a hope.'"
Jeremiah 29:11

FINAL POINTS TO PONDER

- **Do you believe that God has a plan and purpose for your life? Why or why not?**

- **In what areas of your life do you need to trust and depend on God more?**

- **What do you need to cry out to God for today?**

- **How can you move one step closer to God in your life today?**

- **If you are not a believer, but feel that God is calling you into a relationship with Him through Jesus, you need only to cry out to Him and receive His love and forgiveness. Jesus' death on the cross makes this relationship available to all who cry out desperately for Him.**

"For 'Everyone who calls on the name of the Lord will be saved.'"
Romans 10:13

Rick and Chipper one year after the accident

"For everything comes from Him and exists by His power and is intended for His glory. All glory to Him forever! Amen."
Romans 11:36